GOOD COOKING ON A BUDGET

Marguerite Patten

HAMLYN
London · New York · Sydney · Toronto

Published by
The Hamlyn Publishing Group Limited
London · New York · Sydney · Toronto
Hamlyn House, Feltham, Middlesex, England
© Copyright The Hamlyn Publishing Group Limited, 1972
First published 1972
Reprinted 1973

Printed by Litografia A. Romero, S.A.,
Santa Cruz de Tenerife (Spain).
ISBN 0 600 32855 4

The author and publishers thank the following
for their kind co-operation in supplying
colour photographs for this book

American Rice Council, page 31
The British Meat Service, page 23
The Carnation Milk Bureau, page 63
The Dutch Dairy Bureau, page 19
The Flour Advisory Bureau, page 51
Fruit Producers' Council, page 59
Pasta Foods Ltd., cover and pages 27 and 55

CONTENTS

INTRODUCTION

Who can resist a real bargain at sale time? Cooking on a limited budget gives a similar feeling of pleasure and satisfaction, not only in the saving incurred, but in making meals which are just as interesting and colourful as when using more expensive food.

You will see from my recipes that your family can be as well fed on *well chosen* cheaper meat and fish as they would be on prime cuts of meat and luxury fish. After trying the recipes I am sure you will soon become very enthusiastic — and proud of your accomplishments. There are almost unlimited foods that are very reasonable in price, interesting and simple to prepare.

In this book I have set out to give a variety of dishes and menus that will *add interest* to family meals; will give pleasure to the cook, as they are easy to prepare; and will, above all else, ensure adequate food value at a reasonable price.

What are the important requirements for family health?

All the family need adequate amounts of PROTEIN — the food provided in greatest quantity by meat, fish, eggs, cheese, peas, beans, lentils, nuts and milk. This is essential from the time a baby is born. In addition, the meals should provide a certain amount of FAT to create a feeling of warmth, and CARBOHYDRATES (sugar and starch) for energy. Sugar is found not only in all foods that contain this, but in honey, syrup and in most fruits. Starch is in flour, so all foods using flour (bread, cakes, etc.), are a source of this, and so are pasta foods and some vegetables such as potatoes, peas, etc.

The most important vitamins for the family will be provided in the balanced meals in this book, so I am not outlining these.

As you will see, each recipe has a note alongside which suggests a complete menu. I hope this will prove helpful to a busy housewife or whoever is doing the cooking.

It can be annoying to decide upon a certain dish, or meal, and then find you have inadequate time to prepare this properly, so I hope the system of star marking also will be helpful.

☆☆☆　This dish, or the complete menu, quickly prepared and cooked.

☆☆　This dish, or the complete menu, needs over $\frac{3}{4}$ hour, but under 2 hours preparation and cooking.

☆　This dish, or the complete menu, requires over 2 hours preparation and cooking.

Appleade is a delicious drink — pour boiling water over cut-up apples, cool, strain. Add sugar and lemon if liked.

Bacon rinds — fry until crisp, drain and serve with drinks.

Chicken fat from stock etc., and **Meat dripping**, use in cooking. To clarify (clean) — heat with water. Cool, remove fat.

Dandelion leaves, if young, can be shredded and put in salads.

Egg yolks left — cover with a little cold water to prevent a skin forming — use in cooking, for custards, etc.

Filling and topping for sponge — add *slowly* to 1 stiffly beaten egg white, 2 level tablespoons *warmed* sieved jam or jelly.

Grapefruit (and other citrus fruit) **rinds** — use for flavouring. Grate top 'zest', pack in small jars with sugar, or freeze.

Ham — use left-over pieces in scrambled eggs and omelettes.

Ices — made with frozen fruit purées, or juices, are inexpensive.

Jam — goes further as a filling for tarts, etc. — blend with a small quantity of crisp biscuit crumbs or crushed cornflakes.

Kipper fillets (uncooked) — serve as smoked salmon — soak in a little oil, vinegar or lemon juice, and seasoning, for 12 hours.

Leeks — cook carefully to keep whole — serve cold with dressing; hot with butter, as asparagus.

Mushroom stalks — sometimes sold by greengrocers — can be used in many dishes in place of whole mushrooms.

Nuts are expensive — so use wisely — e.g. coat fingers of very fresh bread with jam, or whipped cream, and chopped nuts for 'emergency' cakes; soft cheese and nuts for cocktail savouries.

Oranges — or all citrus fruit — yield more juice if warmed for about 5 minutes in a bowl of hot water.

Pea pods — when young and fresh — cook with stock, onions, etc., sieve to give a delicious soup. Cook *young* broad bean pods as a vegetable, or use in the same way as pea pods for soup.

Quinces — often sold cheaply — add 1 to each 1 lb. apples in pies, etc. Peel and grate the rather hard fruit.

Rarebit (Welsh) — use left-over pieces of Cheddar, Cheshire and other hard cheeses — have a mixture if wished. Blend 4—6 oz. grated or chopped cheese, 1 oz. margarine, seasoning, 2 tablespoons milk or beer, spread on hot toast, brown under grill.

Sugars vary in price — choose granulated for most cooking.

Toad-in-the-hole — a cheap dish — pour pancake batter over hot sausages, etc., in an ovenproof dish. Cook for 30 minutes in a hot oven. Serve at once.

Unfermented apple juice — use as an interesting stock for boiling bacon or chicken. Use half water, half apple juice.

Veal (calf's foot) stewed with vegetables makes a cheap meal — add a little diced stewing steak with the veal, etc., for extra flavour. Cook gently for 2 hours.

Wine — add to stews etc. — tenderises meat. Choose inexpensive wines for cooking, and to drink learn the good bargains.

Xmas pudding — left over — slice, fry in butter, top with sugar.

Yoghourt is one of the most inexpensive foods today — serve with fruit, or flavour with cinnamon or nutmeg.

Zucchini (tiny marrows) also called Courgettes — weigh lightly — do not peel, just wash, slice and fry, or season well and steam.

USEFUL FACTS AND FIGURES

OVEN TEMPERATURES
The following chart gives the conversions from degrees Fahrenheit to degrees Celsius (formerly known as Centigrade) recommended by the manufacturers of electric cookers.

Description	Electric Setting	Gas Mark
very cool	225°F–110°C	$\frac{1}{4}$
	250°F–130°C	$\frac{1}{2}$
cool	275°F–140°C	1
	300°F–150°C	2
very moderate	325°F–170°C	3
moderate	350°F–180°C	4
moderate to	375°F–190°C	5
moderately hot	400°F–200°C	6
hot	425°F–220°C	7
	450°F–230°C	8
very hot	475°F–240°C	9

Note. This table is an approximate guide only. Different makes of cooker vary and if you are in any doubt about the setting, it is as well to refer to the manufacturer's temperature chart.

COMPARISON OF WEIGHTS AND MEASURES
It is useful to note that 3 teaspoons equal 1 tablespoon; the average English teacup is $\frac{1}{4}$ pint; the average English breakfast cup is $\frac{1}{2}$ pint; and when cups are mentioned in recipes they refer to a B.S.I. measuring cup which holds $\frac{1}{2}$ pint or 10 fluid ounces.

It should be noted that the American pint is 16 fluid ounces, as opposed to the British Imperial and Canadian pints which are 20 fluid ounces. The American $\frac{1}{2}$ pint measuring cup is 8 fluid ounces, and is therefore equivalent to $\frac{2}{5}$ British pint. In Australia the British Imperial pint, 20 fluid ounces, is used for liquid measures. Solid ingredients, however, are generally calculated in the American cup measure. In America, standard cup and spoon measurements are used.

METRICATION
For quick and easy reference when buying food, it should be remembered that 1 kilogramme (1000 grammes) equals 2·2 pounds ($35\frac{3}{4}$ ounces) — i.e. as a rough guide, $\frac{1}{2}$ kilogramme is about 1 pound. In liquid measurements 1 litre (10 decilitres or 1000 millilitres) equals almost exactly $1\frac{3}{4}$ pints (1·76), so $\frac{1}{2}$ litre is $\frac{7}{8}$ pint. As a rough guide, therefore, one can assume that the equivalent of 1 pint is a generous $\frac{1}{2}$ litre.

A simple method of converting recipe quantities is to use round figures instead of an exact conversion, taking 25 grammes to 1 ounce, and a generous $\frac{1}{2}$ litre to 1 pint. Since 1 ounce is exactly 28·35 grammes and 1 pint is 568 millilitres, it can be seen that these equivalents will give a slightly smaller finished dish, but the proportion of liquids to solids will remain the same and a satisfactory result will be produced.

The following tables show exact conversions to the nearest whole number, and alongside the recommended amount using the 25 grammes to 1 ounce/$\frac{1}{2}$ litre to 1 pint equivalents.

SOLID AND DRY INGREDIENTS

Imperial	Exact conversion to nearest whole number	Recommended equivalent
Ounces	Grammes	Grammes
1	28	25
2	57	50
3	85	75
4	113	100
5	142	125
6	170	150
7	198	175
8	226	200

LIQUIDS/FLUIDS

Imperial	Exact conversion to nearest whole number	Recommended equivalent
Pints	Millilitres	Litres
1 pint	568	$\frac{1}{2}$ litre-generous
(20 fl. oz)		
$\frac{3}{4}$ pint	426	$\frac{3}{8}$ litre-generous
$\frac{1}{2}$ pint	284	$\frac{1}{4}$ litre-generous
$\frac{1}{4}$ pint	142	$\frac{1}{8}$ litre-generous
(1 fl. oz.	28·4	25 ml)
B.S.I. tablespoon		18 ml
B.S.I. teaspoon		5 ml

In special cases, such as for pastries, it is better to use the more accurate quantities.

MEAL STARTERS

preparation and cooking time

quick ☆☆☆

over ¾ hour but ☆☆
under 2 hours

over 2 hours ☆

A good first course provides not only a more interesting meal, but it can enable you to plan a lighter or more economical main dish.

If you have chosen a cold salad, then the meal starter can be a hot dish; if the main course is based on fish, then a simple meat or egg dish is a good choice. When you have unexpected guests a first course can turn a 'family meal' into a special one; this is why many of the dishes in this chapter can be made from foods in your storecupboard. Suggestions for wise storecupboard 'buys' are given below.

To make interesting and nourishing dishes choose:

Egg dishes: both hot and cold, see pages 60 and 65.

Fish salads and hot fish dishes: remember herrings, mussels, sprats are cheap and equally good in light dishes as in the main course, see pages 26 and 28.

Meat dishes: these should be light in texture, so they do not spoil one's appetite for the main course, see page 36.

Vegetables: both cooked vegetables and salads are ideal and can be given extra food value if you include peas, beans, potatoes, etc. When vegetables such as young spinach are at their best, it is a good idea to serve them as a separate course so that their flavour may be appreciated, see pages 66 and 67.

Fruit juices, etc.: are refreshing, and often provide the vitamin C needed in the menu.

Snacks and canapés, etc.: often a tray of small snacks or a savoury dip (which make excellent use of small portions of 'left over' food) can take the place of a more 'formal' meal starter. Arrange the food on trays, covered with damp paper.

Choosing wisely

These are some of the non-perishable and economical foods to keep in stock; some may be used in main courses, as well as meal starters.

Fish: cod's roes, herring roes, pilchards, pink salmon, sardines, tuna, see pages 11, 12, 35.

Meat: corned beef, luncheon meat and similar meats, inexpensive pâtés, served with salad.

Pasta, etc.: long grain rice, macaroni, spaghetti.

Fruit: grapefruit, orange juice, tomato juice.

Vegetables: baked beans, corn, mixed vegetables.

In addition to the above items it is a good idea to check you have plentiful supplies of:

Eggs: for these can be used in salads and in hot dishes, see page 58.

Cheese: although cheese by itself is rarely served in this country as a 'meal starter', it is excellent used in a cheese sauce over small portions of eggs, fish, etc., see page 33, and as the basis for dips as page 65. Cheddar cheese is undoubtedly the most economical to use, see comments on page 58.

1 small honeydew melon
1 small orange
¼ pint water
2 oz. sugar
pinch ground ginger

to decorate
few mint leaves
few glacé cherries

Melon Cocktail

☆☆☆

Preparation time: 10 minutes
Cooking time: few minutes
Serves 4

Often one can buy quite cheaply a melon that has the mark of the packing container, or is bruised in one place; this method of serving makes it 'go further'. It is also useful when a melon is slightly under-ripe.

Cut the peel thinly from the orange, be careful not to have much white pith, as this gives a bitter syrup. Put the orange peel, water and sugar into a saucepan. Cover tightly and simmer for 10 minutes, then remove the peel. Mix the syrup with the orange juice and ginger. Halve the melon, remove the seeds, and cut the flesh into neat cubes or balls (if you have a vegetable scoop), and put into a bowl. If the melon is ripe, allow the syrup mixture to cool, then pour over the melon; if slightly under-ripe, heat the syrup mixture again until just at boiling point, then pour over the melon. Serve very cold in glasses, and top with mint leaves and/or glacé cherries.

Suggested menu   ☆☆☆
Melon Cocktail
Chicken and Ham Supreme
page 47
Herbed Rice *page 56*
Green Vegetable
Coconut Plum Dumplings
page 74

To vary

a) *Mixed Fruit Cocktail:* add segments of canned or fresh orange, grapefruit, cherries, etc., to the melon.
b) *Wine Melon Cocktail:* use a little less water in the syrup and flavour with white wine, or a rosé or sherry, or omit the orange rind and juice, and make a syrup by heating a generous ¼ pint wine (or a mixture of wine and water) with the sugar. Add ginger if desired.

---

2 grapefruit
2 oz. sultanas
2 tablespoons brown sugar

few drops rum essence
pinch powdered cinnamon
about 1 oz. butter, or margarine

Spiced Sultana Grapefruit

☆☆☆

Preparation time: 10 minutes
Cooking time: 3 minutes
Serves 4

Halve the grapefruit, remove the segments; keep the grapefruit skins intact. Put the sultanas in a basin, cover with a *very little* boiling water. Leave for 5 minutes, then strain off any surplus water. Mix with most of the sugar, the essence, grapefruit segments and cinnamon. Pile back into the grapefruit 'shells'. Spread the butter, or margarine, over the top — with a knife dipped in hot water. Sprinkle with the remainder of the sugar, and brown for 2–3 minutes under a hot grill.

Suggested menu   ☆
Spiced Sultana Grapefruit
Spanish Beef Casserole *page 42*
Jacket Potatoes *page 41*
Green Vegetable
Caramel Pudding *page 75*

To vary

a) Use 2 tablespoons rum instead of rum essence; omit the boiling water. Heat the rum, pour over the sultanas, then add the rest.
b) Heat the grapefruit for 10–15 minutes in a very moderate oven.

⭐⭐ **Rillette of Chicken**

Preparation time: 10 minutes
Cooking time: see method
Serves 3–4

⭐⭐　　**Suggested menu**
Rillette of Chicken
Anchovy Whirls *page 25*
French Peas *page 66*
Duchesse Potatoes *page 67*
Lemon Soufflé *page 73*

giblets from 1 large or 2 smaller
　chickens
1 oz. margarine, or butter
1 clove garlic (optional)
1 pickled gherkin
2 or 3 pickled cocktail onions
　(optional)
1 tablespoon thick cream
　(optional)
1–2 tablespoons chicken stock
　(see method)

seasoning

to garnish
lettuce
lemon

to serve
toast and butter

A Rillette is a very pleasant alternative to a pâté; as it uses meat other than liver, it is often more economical.

If following the recipe for Chicken Pot au Feu, page 48, lift the giblets out of the stock when just tender; it may be you are roasting a chicken, in which case simmer the giblets in well-seasoned water until tender. Lift the giblets out of the liquid, remove the meat from the neck. Chop this and the liver, stomach, and heart, very finely. Do this in a basin (rather than on a chopping board) while the giblets are still warm, so that no meat juices are wasted. Add the margarine or butter, crushed clove of garlic — see sketches describing the way to crush this — diced gherkin and diced onions. Blend well, then add the cream and enough stock (or all the stock) to give a soft consistency. Season well. Allow to become quite cold. Arrange a few lettuce leaves and a wedge of lemon on individual plates. Spoon the Rillette on top. Serve with hot toast and butter.

To vary

a) *Stuffed Eggs:* if the amount of Rillette seems rather small, use as a filling for hard-boiled eggs. Cut the eggs length-ways. Remove the yolks and fill the whites with the chicken mixture. Chop or sieve the yolk and sprinkle over the top.

b) All poultry giblets can be used in the same way, or use equal quantities of lightly cooked lamb's or calf's liver and cooked veal, beef or lamb. Flavour as recipe above.

To crush garlic

Take a segment (called a clove) of garlic from the bulb.

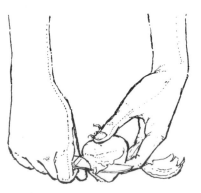

Remove the skin, then place the clove on to a chopping board.

Sprinkle lightly with salt, and crush very firmly with the tip of a good strong knife.

10

8 oz. pig's or lamb's liver
4 oz. streaky bacon, or bacon
    pieces
1 small onion
1 oz. margarine, or chicken fat
1 oz. flour
¼ pint milk
good pinch dried herbs
seasoning

2 tablespoons *fine* soft bread-
    crumbs

to garnish
lettuce

to serve
toast and butter

Liver and Bacon Pâté ☆☆

Preparation time: 15—20 minutes
Cooking time: 1 hour
Serves 4—6

Suggested menu ☆☆
Liver and Bacon Pâté
Cheese and Haddock
Fillets *page 35*
Sauté Potatoes *page 66*
Spinach
Chocolate Soufflé
Pudding *page 73*

Mince the liver, bacon and peeled onion, or, if no mincer is available, chop these very finely. Make a thick sauce of the margarine or fat, flour and milk; add the liver, bacon and onion, and the rest of the ingredients. Beat hard with a wooden spoon — in this way the breadcrumbs become so smooth they are not detected. Put into a greased 1½-pint dish, cover with greased foil, or paper. Stand in a tin of cold water so the pâté does not dry, and cook in the centre of a very moderate oven, 325—350°F., Gas Mark 3—4, for 45 minutes. Keep in the dish until cold and ready to serve; then cut into neat slices, and serve on lettuce with hot toast and butter.

To vary
a) *Garlic Liver Pâté:* add 1 or 2 crushed cloves garlic to the onion, etc.
b) *Tomato Liver Pâté:* use ¼ pint tomato purée from fresh tomatoes, or tomato juice, instead of milk. Add 2 or 3 chopped gherkins to the mixture before baking.

---

1 can sardines in oil
lettuce
2 teaspoons vinegar
½—1 teaspoon made-mustard
seasoning
small piece cucumber

1—2 tablespoons grated Cheddar
    cheese

to garnish
1 or 2 tomatoes

Sardine Salad ☆☆☆

Preparation time: few minutes
Cooking time: none
Serves 2 as a light meal, or
4 as a meal starter

Suggested menu ☆☆
Sardine Salad
Farmhouse Pie *page 61*
Brussels sprouts or other
green vegetable
Date and Apple Crisp *page 76*

Open the can and lift out the sardines, and tip the oil into a basin. Arrange the *well-drained* sardines on lettuce leaves, then blend the vinegar, mustard, and seasoning with the oil. Cut the cucumber (peeled if wished) into matchsticks, mix with the oil, etc., and spoon over the sardines. Sprinkle with the cheese, and garnish with sliced tomatoes.

To vary
a) *Pilchard Salad:* use pilchards in oil, instead of sardines. Cut the fish into 1-inch pieces, then continue as above.
b) *Fresh Sprat Salad:* wash and dry 1 lb. sprats, remove tails and heads. Fry in a little hot fat, drain, season well and use as sardines in salad above.
c) *Smoked Sprat Salad:* these are more expensive, but very good for special occasions. Use as sardines, season well.

Fresh Cod's Roe Pâté

Preparation time: 10 minutes
Cooking time: 15 minutes
Serves 4–6

☆☆☆ **Suggested menu**
Fresh Cod's Roe Pâté
Stuffed Marrow *page 40*
Potato Nests *page 67*
Fresh Fruit

* If using ready-cooked or canned cod's roe there is no cooking time.

8 oz. uncooked cod's roe*
seasoning
2 oz. butter, or margarine
½–1 tablespoon tomato ketchup
few drops anchovy essence
½ lemon

to garnish
lettuce
½ lemon
1–2 tomatoes

to serve
toast and butter

Put the cod's roe into a steamer over a pan of boiling water, season lightly, cover the steamer and cook for 15 minutes, until the roe looks tender and white in colour. Remove the skin from the roe while it is still warm, then mash the roe with a fork. Beat with the butter or margarine, the ketchup, and essence, then add the finely grated rind and juice of the lemon. Taste and add extra seasoning if necessary. Keep in a cool place until ready to serve. Arrange a few lettuce leaves on small plates, top with the cod's roe pâté, and garnish with thin slices of lemon and tomato. Serve with hot toast and butter or, if preferred, French bread.

Note. This pâté is much cheaper than the more familiar smoked cod's roe pâté; this, and the following pâtés, look most attractive served in halved lemon cases.

To vary
a) *Savoury Cod's Roe Pâté:* add 1 or 2 crushed cloves of garlic and 2 teaspoons chopped parsley.
b) *Creamed Cod's Roe Pâté:* use a little less tomato ketchup and add 1–2 tablespoons thick cream.
c) *Herring Roe Pâté:* use herring roes, cooked for 5–6 minutes as above, instead of cod's roe – hard roes are better for this pâté, but if difficult to obtain then buy soft herring roes instead. Cut into tiny pieces, then beat hard with the butter, etc.
d) *Herring Pâté:* use cooked fresh herrings in place of cod's roe. Use rather more lemon to flavour, together with a teaspoon horseradish cream; omit the tomato ketchup.
e) *Kipper Pâté:* cook the kippers lightly, then flake the flesh and proceed as basic resipe; omit the anchovy essence.

Preparing an avocado pear

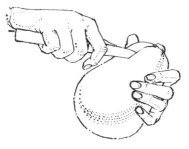

Halve the pear lengthways.

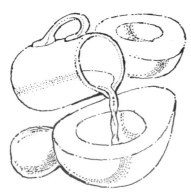

Remove the stone. Fill with French dressing. Serve at once.

In the recipe opposite for Avocado Cream, spoon out the pulp.

Put into a basin with the other ingredients. Blend and put into small bowl or in the avocado halves.

Economy Hors d'oeuvre: these can be made very simply with left over ingredients, for example:
a) Dice cooked sausages, or cold ham, etc.; mix with a little mayonnaise flavoured with mustard. Serve on salad.
b) Arrange left over vegetables in an interesting way on salad, garnish with chopped egg, grated cheese, mayonnaise and chopped watercress or parsley.
c) Serve thinly sliced raw button mushrooms on salad, top with mayonnaise and a little grated cheese. There is no need to skin the mushrooms; wash very well and dry thoroughly.

Anchovy Eggs: hard boil eggs, halve, then remove the yolks and blend with a little butter or mayonnaise, anchovy essence, or chopped anchovy fillets. Serve on salad.

Avocado Cream: make one avocado pear serve four. Remove the skin and mash the pulp with the juice of $\frac{1}{2}$ lemon. Add 2 oz. cream or cottage cheese and 1 tablespoon mayonnaise. Season well. Pile on 4 rounds of buttered bread, and serve on lettuce.
Vary by: (a) adding 3 teaspoons *finely* chopped celery or nuts, (b) substituting 2–3 oz. chopped shrimps, prawns or crab meat for the cheese.

Egg and New Potato Salad: dice 2–3 shelled hard-boiled eggs and 8–12 medium skinned cooked new potatoes. Mix with a little mayonnaise, 2 teaspoons chopped parsley and 1 teaspoon capers. Pile on to lettuce, garnish with chopped parsley and sliced tomato. Serves 4.

New Potato Dip: scrub, but do not scrape, tiny new potatoes; either boil in salted water or fry until crisp. Serve very hot with Tartare sauce, page 52, as a dip.

Orange and Grapefruit Cocktail: an excellent way to 'eke-out' either fruit. Cut away the peel from fresh oranges and grapefruit and divide into segments, or use canned fruit. Arrange alternate layers in grapefruit glasses. Flavour with (a) sprigs of fresh mint and sugar, or (b) a little white wine or sherry, or (c) put the fruit into shallow individual ovenproof dishes, sprinkle with brown sugar and grated nutmeg, heat in the oven or under the grill until the sugar melts, then serve hot.

Tomato and Pepper Salad: slice tomatoes and cut rings of green pepper (remove core and seeds from the pepper). Arrange on lettuce. Top with oil and vinegar dressing, chopped parsley and chives.

Tuna Shells: roll out 4 oz. short crust pastry *very thinly* and line 4–5 scallop shells (a fishmonger will let you have these). Prick well and bake 'blind' in a hot oven for 12–15 minutes, until crisp and golden. Keep warm. Heat 1 oz. margarine and 3 tablespoons milk, add a medium can of flaked tuna, 2 beaten eggs, seasoning, and cook gently until the eggs just set. Lift pastry from the shells, fill with the fish mixture, garnish with parsley and lemon. Serves 4–5.
If serving cold, allow pastry to cool and blend 1–2 tablespoons mayonnaise with the egg mixture, so it is not too stiff. Serve on lettuce and garnish with lemon. Mashed pilchards, well drained pink salmon, or sardines, can be used instead of tuna.

SOUPS

preparation and cooking time

quick ☆☆☆

over ¾ hour but ☆☆
under 2 hours

over 2 hours ☆

Home-made soups give a feeling of 'well being' to a family menu. Often a satisfying soup can form the basis of a complete light meal, with a salad or cheese, etc. In warm weather choose an unthickened soup to serve cold. Many soups depend upon good stock; it is sensible to simmer bones to make this *if you have a refrigerator, or will use it quickly*. When you have no bones the modern stock cubes are invaluable. Choose beef stock cubes for 'meaty' soups, and chicken or more delicate-flavoured cubes for fish or vegetable soups. To save time *grate* the vegetables. Some interesting soups one can produce in minutes are:

a) *Vegetable tomato consommé:* grate peeled carrots and/or potatoes into canned tomato juice, and cook until the vegetables are tender. Finely chopped spring onions, or a very little grated onion and crushed garlic, may be added. Serve hot topped with grated cheese, or cold with natural yoghourt.

b) *Corn Chowder:* fry 2–3 rashers chopped streaky bacon (or buy bacon pieces). Add 1–2 grated onions and cook for several minutes, then add approximately 1¼ pints chicken stock. Cook for 10 minutes until the onions are nearly soft. Add a small or medium can of corn. Heat thoroughly. Serve hot, topped with chopped parsley.

c) *Ham and Green Pea Chowder:* fry 2–3 grated onions in a knob of fat. Add about 1¼ pints stock (from cooking bacon or chicken), and simmer for 10 minutes. Add a small can of peas, or small packet frozen peas. Heat thoroughly. Add a pinch of sugar, and a little chopped mint, and top with snippets of cooked ham, and bread croûtons, just before serving hot.

Choosing wisely

These are some of the foods that make good cheap soups.

Fish: these soups are less usual or not so popular as others, but they make an excellent light meal. Choose cod, fresh haddock, mussels, etc., see pages 18 and 32, and make fish stock with the skin, bones and head of fish.

Meat: ham and bacon provide excellent flavours and food value for soup. *Never* waste bacon rinds; use these to add to soups.

Vegetables: root vegetables make excellent soups, the first recipe on page 17 a) is a good basic one. Spring and summer vegetables (young peas, and pea pods, cucumber, etc.) are less usual, but make soups from these when possible, see the Curried Cucumber Soup on page 16.

Fruits: although fruit soups are rare, they *will* become popular when you serve them, for they are so refreshing, see the Orange and Apple Soup on page 21.

Top soups with interesting garnishes to make them *look* as good as they taste, see page 20. Chopped fresh herbs can be added to the soup, or a *bouquet garni* (bunch of mixed herbs) can be cooked with the soup, and removed just before serving.

½ marrow bone, or bones from
   joint of beef
1½ pints water
seasoning

bouquet garni
2 onions
2 carrots
2 oz. long grain rice

Beef Broth ☆☆

Preparation time: few minutes
Cooking time: 1½ hours, or
see method
Serves 4–6

Suggested menu ☆☆
Beef Broth
Seafood Pie *page 35*
Green Vegetable
Fruit Cups *page 78*

Put the bones into a saucepan with the water, seasoning and *bouquet garni*. Bring the water to the boil and remove any grey bubbles from the surface; cover the pan and simmer for a minimum of 1 hour, or cook in a covered casserole for a slightly longer period, using the oven on a low heat, or allow about 25–30 minutes at 15 lb. pressure, in a pressure pan. Peel and chop the onions and carrots finely. Remove the bones from the stock (strain this if it appears too cloudy and return to the pan). Add the vegetables and rice, and cook for a further 20 minutes. Remove the herbs, taste and add extra seasoning if necessary.

To vary
a) When bones are not available, use beef stock cubes, or yeast or beef extract, to give you the basic stock.
b) To make a more filling soup, add 4–6 oz. minced raw beef, and simmer for about 40 minutes in the stock, or add minced cooked meat and heat thoroughly. This makes the kind of soup that 'makes a meal' if followed by cheese and biscuits.
c) Put about 2 oz. pasta (elbow length macaroni, noodles, etc.) into the soup instead of rice.
d) *Flemish Beef Soup:* omit the rice or pasta, and before adding the vegetables put a large slice of crustless bread, spread with made-mustard (French or English), into the soup. Cook for 5 minutes, then stir briskly to break this. Add the vegetables. The bread gives a slightly thickened soup.
e) *Beef Soup with Savoury Dumplings:* make the basic soup but omit the rice. Cook the stock, then remove the bones. Meanwhile, sieve 2 oz. self-raising flour with good pinch salt, pepper, dry mustard and curry powder. Add 1 oz. shredded suet, 1 teaspoon chopped parsley, and bind with water. Form into tiny balls the size of a hazelnut. Put the onion and carrot into the stock, cook for about 5 minutes, then add the dumplings and cook for a further 12–15 minutes.

Preparing a bouquet garni

Take a sprig of each or some of the following:
parsley, thyme (lemon thyme is ideal), sage – not essential as this has a very strong flavour – chives (optional), majoram, bay leaf, mace.
Tie with fine cotton and put into sauces or stews; remove before serving.

Remember you can buy small bags of dried herbs.

Curried Cucumber Soup

1 medium onion
1 medium cucumber
1½ oz. butter, margarine, or chicken fat
1–2 teaspoons curry powder
1 pint chicken stock (see method)
¼ pint yoghourt
seasoning
good pinch sugar

Preparation time: 10 minutes
Cooking time: 20 minutes
Serves 4–6

☆☆☆ **Suggested menu**
Curried Cucumber Soup
Chicken and Almonds *page 49*
Savoury Rice *page 56*
Broccoli
Ice Cream Sundae *page 78*

Peel the onion and *most* of the cucumber, and chop into small pieces. Put the small piece of cucumber, *with* the peel, on one side for garnish. Heat the butter or other fat, and toss the onion and cucumber in this for 5 minutes. Stir the curry powder into the vegetables, then add the stock. Bring to the boil and cook for about 15 minutes. Sieve, or put into a warmed blender and emulsify; if too thick a purée, add a little extra stock. Reheat to serve hot – add the yoghourt, seasoning and sugar just before serving; or allow the purée to cool and then add the yoghourt, etc. Top with wafer thin slices of cucumber.

To vary
a) Omit the curry powder and use thin cream instead of yoghourt; a *bouquet garni* can be put in with the cucumber as it cooks.
b) Use bottled or canned tomato juice in place of stock; use only a pinch of curry powder.

Speedy Rolls

8 oz. self-raising flour (or plain flour and 2 level teaspoons baking powder)
good pinch salt
½–1 oz. margarine
milk, or milk and water to mix

Preparation time: 5 minutes
Cooking time: 15 minutes
Makes 8 rolls

☆☆ **Suggested menu**
Curried Vegetable Soup
page 17
Speedy Rolls
Polish Chicken Salad *page 49*
Apple Puffs *page 69*

Sieve the flour, or flour and baking powder, and salt, rub in the small amount of margarine and mix to a *slightly* sticky consistency with the milk, or milk and water. Divide into 8 portions. Flour your hands fairly well, and roll each portion into a neat ball. Bake on an ungreased baking tray above the centre of a hot oven, 425°F., Gas Mark 6–7, until firm and pale golden.

To vary
a) Add 1–2 oz. finely grated Cheddar cheese to the flour. An excellent way of using very stale cheese.
b) Blend ½ teaspoon Marmite with 4 tablespoons milk. Use this to mix the dough, then add any extra liquid required.

To shape rolls

2 medium carrots
1 small turnip
2 small onions
2 medium potatoes
1 oz. fat, or margarine
1 level tablespoon flour
1–2 teaspoons curry powder

1¼ pints water, or white stock
seasoning
pinch sugar

to garnish
chopped parsley

Peel and grate the vegetables coarsely, or dice neatly. (Leave the potatoes until last, so they do not discolour.) Heat the fat or margarine, and add in the flour and curry powder. Stir over a low heat for several minutes, then add the water or stock gradually. Stir as you do so (or bring the liquid to the boil, then whisk sharply), so you have a smooth thin sauce. Add the vegetables, season lightly, put in the sugar and cook for about 10 minutes, if grated; or 15–20 minutes if diced. Taste and add more seasoning if required. Top with chopped parsley.

To vary
a) Omit curry powder. Flavour with a good pinch of dried mixed herbs, or 1–2 teaspoons chopped fresh herbs.
b) Sieve the soup when cooked and reheat.
c) Top any version of the soup with grated cheese, or yoghourt, or a little cream cheese, just before serving. This makes it a more nourishing dish.
d) Add a few canned or cooked haricot or butter beans, and/or peas. Heat well.
e) *Lentil and Vegetable Soup:* soak 2 oz. lentils in 1½ pints stock for several hours. Add the lentils and stock to the fat and flour (or flour and curry powder) as basic recipe, above. Bring to the boil and then season; lower the heat and simmer for about 45 minutes. Add grated or diced vegetables, and continue as recipe above. Lentils provide protein to the meal.

Curried Vegetable Soup ☆☆

Preparation time: 15–20 minutes
Cooking time: 20–30 minutes
Serves 4

Suggested menu ☆☆
Curried Vegetable Soup
Polish Chicken Salad *page 49*
Speedy Rolls *page 16*
Apple Puffs *page 69*

---

about 8 spring onions
about 8 oz. cooked beetroot
1¼ pints beef stock, or water
  and 2 stock cubes

1 teaspoon vinegar
seasoning
5 oz. carton yoghourt

Chop the onions and part of the stems of the onions. Skin, and grate the beetroot coarsely. Put into the stock, bring to the boil. Simmer for 10 minutes, add vinegar and seasoning. Serve hot or cold topped with yoghourt.

To vary
a) Use 4 oz. cranberries and 1 tablespoon sugar, instead of beetroot. Simmer until tender (15 minutes).
b) Use raw beetroot, 1–2 finely chopped onions, and carrots. Simmer for 1½–2 hours in 2 pints beef stock, proceed as above.

Quick Beetroot Bortsch ☆☆☆

Preparation time: 15 minutes
Cooking time: 15 minutes
Serves 4–6

Suggested menu ☆☆☆
Quick Beetroot Bortsch
Kebabs *page 38*
Potato Crisps, or Savoury Rice *page 56*
Pain Perdu *page 78*

Haddock Soup

☆☆☆

Preparation time: 20 minutes
Cooking time: 25 minutes
Serves 4–6

☆☆☆ **Suggested menu**
Haddock Soup
Corned Beef Hash *page 40*
Sliced Beetroot
Glazed Fruit Fool *page 78*

8 oz. smoked haddock (fillet or whole fish)
bouquet garni
pepper
grated rind 1 lemon
1 onion

1 oz. margarine
1 level tablespoon cornflour
½ pint milk

to garnish
lemon, parsley

Cut the haddock into pieces (this is a good way to use part of a whole smoked haddock). Put into a pan; include bones, tail, etc. Cover with cold water, and bring the water to the boil. Remove the fish, flake finely, put on one side. Return bones and skin to the water with the *bouquet garni*, shake of pepper, and grated lemon rind; simmer for 10 minutes to give a stronger stock; strain the liquid; add enough water if necessary to give ¾ pint. Meanwhile chop the onion finely, or grate this and fry in hot margarine. Blend the cornflour with the milk. Add to the onion, together with the fish stock, bring to the boil and stir until thickened. Put in the flaked fish and heat for a few minutes. Garnish with tiny pieces of lemon and chopped parsley.

To vary

a) Use any other white fish or shell fish. In this case you will need salt as well as pepper.
b) Follow the recipe for Creamed Mussels page 32, add extra milk to give a thinner consistency, and serve as a soup.

Tomato Lentil Soup

Preparation time: 15 minutes, plus overnight soaking
Cooking time: 1 hour
Serves 6–8

☆☆ **Suggested menu**
Tomato Lentil Soup
Cheese and Vegetable Flan
page 62
Duchesse Potatoes *page 67*
Green Salad *page 66*
Stuffed Baked Apples *page 78*

3 oz. lentils
2 pints ham stock, or water and a few bacon rinds (see method)

1 lb. tomatoes
seasoning
bouquet garni

Wash the lentils in cold water. Drain well, then put into a basin or saucepan. Cover with the stock, or water and bacon rinds, and leave for about 12 hours. Add the chopped tomatoes to the lentils and stock, season lightly, put in the *bouquet garni* of herbs. Simmer for just about 1 hour. Sieve, then return to the pan, thin down with extra stock if required, and reheat. Add extra seasoning if wished.

Note. This is a very filling soup, but is excellent when frozen and reheated, so it is worth cooking a generous amount.

To vary

a) Use dried peas in place of lentils.
b) Add 2 chopped onions to the mixture.
c) Add a little thin cream to the soup.
d) Skin the tomatoes before adding to the lentils, etc., and put the soup into a warmed liquidiser and emulsify, instead of sieving.
e) Flavour the soup with 1–2 teaspoons curry powder, and add 1–2 oz. margarine when reheating after sieving, to give a richer texture.

Stuffed Herrings, Cheese Potato Balls, see pages 28 and 65

☆☆☆ **Potato Soup**

Preparation time: 15 minutes
Cooking time: 18–20 minutes
Serves 4–5

☆☆ **Suggested menu**
Potato Soup
Minced Beef Provençal
page 43
Sprouts, or other green
vegetable
Banana Fritters *page 70*

2 large onions
1 oz. margarine, or chicken fat
1 pint chicken or ham stock,
  or water and 1 chicken
  stock cube only

1 lb. old potatoes
seasoning

to garnish
chopped parsley, or watercress

Peel the onions, then grate coarsely and toss in the hot margarine, or fat, for about 5 minutes, lowering the heat so they do not brown. Add the stock, or water and stock cube, and bring to the boil. Peel and wash the potatoes, and grate coarsely. Put into the stock as soon as they are grated to prevent their discolouring. Add seasoning. Cook fairly quickly for about 8–10 minutes, until the potatoes are tender. Serve at once, topped with parsley or watercress.

To vary

a) *New Potato Soup:* use a small bunch chopped spring onions (the white bulbs and some green stalks) instead of large onions; cook as above, then add about 12 oz. new potatoes, scraped and cut into very small cubes. Flavour the soup with a sprig of mint as it cooks. Top with paprika pepper before serving.

b) *Carrot Potato Soup:* use 8 oz. carrots and 8 oz. potatoes, instead of all potatoes. If the vegetables are old, grate as basic recipe; if young then dice as variation a).

c) *Potato Leek Soup:* use sliced leeks in place of onions.

d) *Vichyssoise Soup:* use leeks in place of onions. The vegetables may be cut into pieces; when they are tender, rub the soup through a sieve. Stir a little cream into the mixture, also a little white wine, if desired. This soup is delicious served very cold, topped with chopped chives.

To serve with soups

1. Croûtons: cut toasted bread into dice or dice fresh bread, fry in deep or shallow fat and drain on absorbent paper.

3. Nuts: sprinkle salted peanuts on chicken or curry soups.

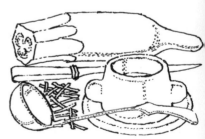

5. Sprinkle 'matchsticks' of ham and/or cucumber on soup.

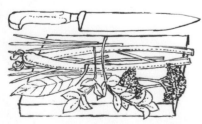

2. Herbs, etc.: chopped parsley, chives, spring onions, etc., to sprinkle on the soup.

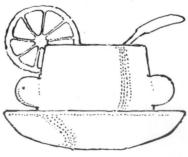

4. Fruit: slit slices of lemon, balance on the soup cups.

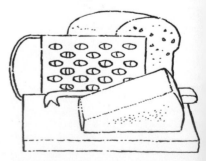

6. Cheese gratinée: top vegetable soups with grated cheese on rounds of bread. Brown under the grill.

1 lb. cooking apples
2 oranges
¾ pint water

2 oz. sugar
nutmeg

Orange and Apple Soup

☆☆☆

Preparation time: 20 minutes
Cooking time: 20 minutes
Serves 4

If you are sieving the soup do not peel the apples, but if you intend to use a liquidiser remove the peel and cores. Slice the apples, and put into a pan with the *finely grated* orange rind and water. Simmer steadily until a soft purée; sieve or emulsify in the warmed liquidiser goblet. Add the sugar while the soup is warm to dissolve this, then stir in the orange juice. Taste the soup, it should be fairly 'sharp', but if too sour add a little more sugar. Serve hot or cold, topped with grated nutmeg.

Suggested menu ☆☆☆
Orange and Apple Soup
Chicken and Beef Cream
page 47
Carrots, peas and mashed
potatoes, or salad
Cheese and biscuits, or
Speedy Rolls *page 16*

To vary

a) *Cider Apple Soup:* use half water and half dry or sweet cider; adjust the amount of sugar accordingly.

b) *Lemon Apple Soup:* use 1 large lemon in place of 2 oranges plus a little extra water.

c) *Cherry Soup, etc.:* use cooking cherries *if* cheap (they are generally rather expensive), or cherry plums, or other rather 'tart' fruit.

d) *Curried Fruit Cucumber Soup:* this unusual combination is delicious served cold in hot weather. Make the orange and apple soup, as above, but add 2 teaspoons curry powder to the fruit in cooking. Sieve or emulsify, and cool, then blend with 4–5 tablespoons finely diced cucumber. Put into soup cups and top with natural yoghourt and finely chopped parsley and chopped chives.

---

2 lemons
1½ pints chicken stock, or use
    water and 2 chicken stock
    cubes

2 level tablespoons semolina
little parsley
seasoning

Lemon Soup

☆☆☆

Preparation time: 6–8 minutes
Cooking time: 15–20 minutes
Serves 4–6

Grate the rind from the lemons and squeeze out the juice. Bring the chicken stock or water and stock cubes, to the boil. Add the lemon rind. Sprinkle the semolina on to the boiling liquid, whisking hard as you do so. Simmer gently for 10 minutes; stirring from time to time. Add the lemon juice, a little chopped parsley, plenty of seasoning, and heat thoroughly. Pour into soup bowls or soup cups, and top with more chopped parsley.

Suggested menu ☆☆☆
Lemon Soup
Fish Caesar Salad *page 34*
Devilled Potato Salad *page 66*
Gooseberry Creams *page 73*

To vary

a) Serve this as a cold soup. Cook as above, allow to cool, then add about ¼ pint thin cream. Garnish with chopped watercress instead of parsley.

b) Add 1–2 finely chopped or grated onions to the stock, and cook with the semolina. Reduce the lemons from 2 to 1.

Penny-wise Ideas for Soups

Cream soups: when any soup recipe suggests adding cream, use the top of the milk or the cheaper single cream, i.e. thin cream.

Wine in soups: where a recipe suggests adding sherry, etc., substitute the cheaper white wines, or dry cider, instead.

Use stock wisely: never waste a good stock; make it the basis of a soup — see ideas below. If it is lacking in flavour add a little yeast extract, or Worcestershire sauce, or a stock cube.

Vegetable soups: most left over vegetables may be sieved, or put into a liquidiser with stock, or stock and milk, and made into a purée for soup. To give additional flavour and food value, top with grated cheese. Less usual vegetables make excellent soups, e.g. cucumber — so use these when plentiful and cheap.

Chicken Vegetable Soup: cook extra vegetables in chicken stock as suggested on page 48, or make stock from chicken bones and/or giblets, and cook vegetables in this. Sieve the vegetables, or put into the liquidiser and emulsify with a little stock, until a smooth purée. Return to the pan with enough stock to make the consistency of thin cream. Season well and heat. If preferred, blend a little cream or white sauce with the soup.

Clear Chicken Consommé: make a good stock from cooking a chicken as page 48, or from chicken bones. Strain through a fine sieve or muslin, and reheat with plenty of seasoning, a tablespoon finely chopped parsley and/or chopped chives. To make the soup more sustaining see suggestions under Beef broth, page 15, i.e. add vegetables, pasta or rice, etc.

Spinach Soup: make a thin sauce with 1 oz. margarine, 1 oz. flour, 1 pint milk, or $\frac{1}{2}$ pint milk and $\frac{1}{2}$ pint chicken stock. Add either a small packet frozen uncooked chopped spinach, or 6–8 oz. sieved cooked spinach, and heat thoroughly. Flavour with plenty of seasoning and grated nutmeg, and blend in 2–3 tablespoons single cream before serving. To give additional flavour, simmer 1–2 chopped or grated onions in the liquid before adding the spinach.

Watercress Soup: as spinach soup, but make the sauce with stock and milk; flavour with the finely grated rind of 1–2 lemons. Add about 4–5 generously filled tablespoons chopped watercress, and simmer for a few minutes only. Top with grated cheese before serving.

To make canned soups go further: canned soups will give more portions if you

a) simmer 1 large diced potato in $\frac{1}{2}$ pint stock, or water flavoured with yeast or beef extract. When soft add to any meat soups or to Mulligatawny soup.

b) fry 1 or 2 grated onions and any tiny pieces of bacon in a small knob of fat until the onions are soft. Add $\frac{1}{4}$ pint milk, or milk and water. Mix with cream soups.

c) crush a clove of garlic, grate a potato and carrot and onion, then toss in a small knob of fat. Add $\frac{1}{2}$ pint water, season well and simmer with a few chopped fresh herbs or pinch dried herbs. Excellent to 'eke out' most soups.

Top: Herbed Lamb and Tomato Stew, see page 42
Bottom: Spanish Beef Casserole, see page 42

FISH

preparation and cooking time

quick ☆☆☆

over ¾ hour but ☆☆
under 2 hours

over 2 hours ☆

Fish is one of the protein foods needed by all the family. As it is easy to digest it is an ideal food for evening meals, for young children, and the elderly. Many fish are expensive, but, on the other hand, you will find a good selection of the cheaper fish available during most months of the year. Do not be conservative in the way you cook fish; frying is one of the favourite methods for most people, but grilled fish retains as much flavour, uses less fat and is, in consequence, more digestible.

Serve fish in interesting sauces: often you can use a concentrated soup as a sauce, to save time, see page 33.

Use small quantities of fish for a filling in pancakes and omelettes, and in the favourite fish cakes, croquettes, etc. Recipes for all these dishes are in this chapter.

Fish stews are less usual, but they are an ideal way of combining fish and interesting vegetables; so are patties and fish pies.

Stale fish is not only a waste of money, it is a dangerous food to serve, so buy fish carefully. Fresh fish of all kinds should have a bright look to the skin and scales; the eyes should look bright. If fish has an unpleasant smell of ammonia then it is stale.

When a particular fresh fish is out of season, or during the winter when storms at sea make fish much more expensive, it is wise to choose frozen or canned fish instead. Many varieties of the cheaper fish are obtainable frozen or canned. Some suggestions for less expensive fish are given below.

Choosing wisely
White fish: this is probably the most adaptable of all fish, for it can be cooked in all the basic ways, and used in 'made-up' dishes too. The cheaper white fish to choose are: cod, flounder (when in season, but these are fairly full of bone), fresh haddock, huss, plaice (when in season), rock salmon. Use cod's roe and herring roes too, for interesting and nutritious snacks and main meals.

Oily fish: as these fish are full of flavour they can be cooked in simple ways. Choose fresh herrings (best when NOT too full of roe), sprats. (Serve with Horseradish or Mustard sauce.)

Shell fish: these are the more luxury fish, but small quantities of prawns and shrimps help to turn plain dishes into exciting ones. Mussels, cockles and occasionally scallops can be economical though; recipes pages 18, 26, 32.

Smoked fish: bloaters, buckling, haddock, kippers, sprats, are excellent for light dishes.

Canned fish: herrings, pilchards, sardines, are useful standbys in the cupboard, and although anchovy fillets are not cheap, a small quantity 'goes a long way'.

4 medium, or 8 small, fillets
  whiting or plaice*
pot anchovy paste
pepper
1 oz. margarine

2 tablespoons milk

to garnish
parsley and/or lemon

* choose smaller fillets for an hors d'oeuvre, and serve one per person.

Spread each fillet with anchovy paste, season lightly with pepper, then roll the fish. Spread half the margarine at the bottom of an overproof dish. Put the fillets in the dish, add the rest of the margarine and milk. Cover with greased foil or greaseproof paper to give a softer texture to the fish; if preferred, leave uncovered and the fish will be a little harder on the outside. Bake for 20–25 minutes in the centre of a moderate oven, 375°F., Gas Mark 4–5. Garnish with parsley and lemon.

To vary
a) Choose other fish pastes, or mix 2–3 left over mashed sardines, or 4–6 chopped anchovy fillets, with 2–3 tablespoons *fine* soft breadcrumbs, seasoning, and a few drops vinegar.
b) Use veal (parsley and thyme), sage and onion, or rice stuffing — page 52.
c) Mix ¼ pint thick cheese, anchovy, or other sauce, see Note (1) page 33, with a little chopped gherkin or cucumber, or a few chopped prawns or other shell fish, or flaked canned salmon or tuna.
d) Roll each fillet round half a well-seasoned skinned tomato.
e) Fry 1 rasher bacon, chop finely and mix with 1–2 skinned chopped tomatoes, 2 teaspoons finely chopped raw onion, 2 tablespoons fine breadcrumbs, and seasoning.

Anchovy Whirls

Preparation time: 5 minutes
Cooking time: 20–25 minutes
Serves 4 as a main course

Suggested menu ☆☆
Rillette of Chicken *page 10*
Anchovy Whirls
French Peas *page 66*
Duchesse Potatoes *page 67*
Lemon Soufflé *page 73*

To roll fish

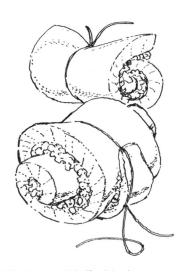

Skin fish if wished, see page 30.
Put filling on fish.

Roll like this, and tie if wished.

Cockle Chowder

Preparation time: 15 minutes
Cooking time: 25 minutes
Serves 4–6

☆☆☆ **Suggested menu**
Cockle Chowder
Cheese, rolls, butter
Tomatoes and/or celery
Fresh Fruit

Although this is a type of soup; it is so filling that I have put it among fish main dishes.

2–3 rashers streaky bacon
1 oz. margarine
1 large onion
$\frac{1}{2}$ pint water
2 large potatoes
seasoning
bouquet garni
$\frac{1}{4}$ pint milk
1–1$\frac{1}{2}$ pints cockles

to garnish
paprika pepper
chopped parsley

to serve
4–6 rounds of French bread
    or toast

Cut the bacon into small pieces. Put into a saucepan with the margarine and bacon rinds. Heat for a few minutes, then add the finely chopped or grated onion. Continue cooking for 2–3 minutes. Add the water, and bring this to the boil. Peel and dice the potatoes, put into the boiling water. Season lightly, add the herbs, (the *bouquet garni*), and cook for 8–10 minutes until the potatoes are *almost* soft. Remove the herbs and bacon rinds. Add the milk and cockles; heat gently for a further 5 minutes. Meanwhile put the bread or toast into 4–6 soup bowls, or plates. Pour over the chowder. Garnish with paprika and parsley.

To vary

a) *Mussel Chowder:* use 2/3 pints mussels instead of cockles. To prepare mussels, scrub well. If any shells are open tap sharply. If they do not close, discard the fish. Put the mussels into a large saucepan. Add about $\frac{1}{2}$ pint water, seasoning, and a *bouquet garni* or bunch parsley Bring the water to the boil and heat gently until the shells open. Lift out the mussels; cool enough to handle; throw away any that have not opened. Remove the fish from one or both shells (some recipes suggest mussels are served on one shell); also cut away the small weed. Use the liquid in which the mussels were cooked as the liquid in the chowder. Serves 4–6.

b) *Scallop Chowder:* when scallops are inexpensive buy 4–6. Remove from the shells, cut into neat pieces. Add to the bacon and potato mixture (with the milk) 8 minutes before serving the soup, to make certain the scallops are cooked. Serves 4–6.

Cockles

Mussels

Scallops

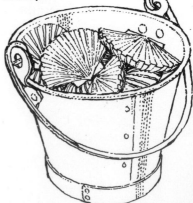

26

Minced Beef Provençal, see page 43

Stuffed Herrings

Preparation time: 20 minutes
Cooking time: see method
Serves 4

Suggested menu
Stuffed Herrings
Potato Salad *page 66*
Tomato Salad *page 66*
Halfpay Pudding *page 74*

See picture, *page 19*

4 herrings
seasoning
½ oz. margarine

for the stuffing
1 egg
2 oz. Edam cheese
2 oz. canned or cooked corn
  (off the cob)

1 tablespoon grated onion, or
  chopped spring onions
1—2 tablespoons French
  dressing see page 52

to garnish
¼ lettuce
cucumber

Remove the heads, and bone the herrings as illustrations below, use the roes for a separate savoury, see Fish in Savoury Custard page 35. Wash and dry the fish and season lightly. Either bake for about 20—25 minutes towards the top of a moderately hot oven, or grill the fish until tender. Do not over-cook.

The herrings should be covered with the margarine and foil if baking, or brushed with the melted margarine if being grilled. Hard boil and chop the egg, while the fish cooks and cools. Grate the cheese, then mix all the stuffing ingredients together. Fill the fish, and arrange on a dish; garnish with shredded lettuce, cucumber slices, or wedges of lemon.

To bone herrings

1
Cut off the heads and split the herring along the stomach.

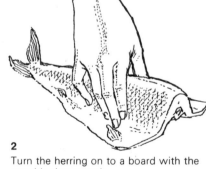

2
Turn the herring on to a board with the cut side downwards.

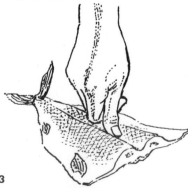

3
Run your **thumb hard** along the centre; this loosens the back bone.

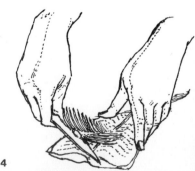

4
Turn the fish over: you will find the back bones, plus the little bones attached, can be lifted away from the flesh with a sharp knife.

3–4 medium tomatoes
4 herrings
6–8 medium potatoes

2–3 medium onions
1½ oz. margarine
seasoning

Herring Bake

Skin the tomatoes and slice fairly thinly. Bone the herrings as page 28; cut each herring into 2 fillets. Peel the potatoes and onions; cut into *wafer thin* slices. Grease a 2-pint casserole with some of the margarine, and put in one-third of the potatoes, season, and add half the onions, tomatoes and herring fillets; *season each layer* lightly. Next put in *half* the remaining potatoes, *all* the tomatoes, first, then the herrings, the onions, and finally a neat topping of potato slices. Cover with tiny pieces of margarine; bake in the centre of a very moderate to moderate oven, 350–375°F., Gas Mark 4–5, until the vegetables and fish are tender and the top layer of potatoes crisp and golden brown.

Preparation time: 25 minutes
Cooking time: 45–50 minutes
Serves 4–6

Suggested menu ☆☆
Herring Bake
Jacket Potatoes *page 41*
Spinach
Gypsy Tart *page 77*

To vary
a) *Fish Bake:* use small pieces of skinned cod, haddock, whiting or plaice, instead of herrings. As these fish are less oily than herrings brush over with melted margarine.
b) *Bacon Bake:* use diced uncooked streaky bacon in place of the fish.

1 small onion
1 clove garlic (optional)
4 portions fresh haddock
2 oz. margarine
small can tomatoes

4 tablespoons water
seasoning
2 teaspoons capers (optional)
2–3 teaspoons chopped parsley

Haddock Belle Bretonne ☆☆☆

Peel, and chop or grate the onion, and crush the clove of garlic. Fry the haddock in the hot margarine for 2–3 minutes, turn and fry for the same time on the second side. Lift out of the frying pan on to a plate. Put the onion and garlic into the frying pan, and fry in any margarine left after cooking the fish. Add the tomatoes, water, seasoning and capers. Simmer for about 5 minutes, then replace the pieces of haddock and heat thoroughly. Lift the fish and sauce on to a serving dish, and top with the parsley.

Preparation time: 10 minutes
Cooking time: 15 minutes
Serves 4

Suggested menu ☆☆☆
Haddock Belle Bretonne
Fresh, frozen, or canned, peas, or green vegetable
Creamed Potatoes, use fresh or instant potatoes
Orange Fritters *page 70*

To vary
a) Add chopped anchovy fillets to the tomato mixture, for special occasions.
b) Use other white fish in place of haddock.
c) When fresh tomatoes are cheap, use 4–5 large chopped tomatoes (skinned if wished) and about ¼ pint water, in place of the canned tomatoes and 4 tablespoons water. Simmer the tomatoes with the water for about 10 minutes before adding the fish.

Cod Caprice

Preparation time: 15 minutes
Cooking time: 10 minutes
Serves 4

 Suggested menu
Cod Caprice
Creamed Spinach *page 66*
Potatoes
Custard Cream *page 78*

12 oz.–1 lb. cod fillet
2–3 tablespoons milk
seasoning
1½ oz. flour

2–3 oz. fat
2 large firm bananas

to garnish
watercress

Skin the cod, see below (unless using frozen skinless cod, in which case there is no need to defrost the fish). Cut into 8 fingers, brush with milk, and coat with a good layer of the seasoned flour. Fry in hot fat until crisp and golden brown. Drain on absorbent paper and keep hot. Prepare the bananas while the fish is frying; peel, halve and split each half. Coat in seasoned flour and fry in the fat remaining in the pan. Arrange the bananas on the fish and garnish with watercress.

To vary:
a) Use ready coated frozen fish, or fish fingers.
b) *Cod Indienne:* use the recipe above but add 1–2 teaspoons curry powder to the flour. Serve with chutney, as well as the bananas.
c) *Paprika Cod:* use the recipe above and add 1 teaspoon paprika to the flour. Serve with the bananas and a white sauce flavoured with paprika, see page 33.

Cod Kebabs

Preparation time: 5 minutes
Cooking time: 6–8 minutes

Suggested menu
Beef Broth *page 15*
Cod Kebabs
Green Salad
Compôte of Fruit *page 71*

2 fillets cod, about 1 inch thick
seasoning

3–4 rashers streaky bacon
1 oz. margarine

Skin the fillets of cod and cut the fish into 1-inch cubes; season. Remove the rinds from the bacon, and cut each rasher into 3 or 4 pieces. Roll these. Melt the margarine. Put the pieces of cod and bacon rolls on to long metal skewers. Brush the fish with the margarine, and grill until cooked and golden brown. Tiny tomatoes, mushrooms, etc., may be added, as page 38.

To skin fish

Choose a really sharp knife. Make a slit at one end of the fish fillet or tail end of a whole fish.

Dip the blade of the knife in salt (this helps to cut away the flesh) and begin to cut the fish from the skin.

Continue easing the fish away from the skin – do not pull otherwise you break the flesh.

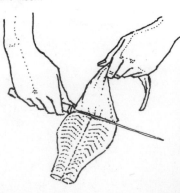

30

Beef and Rice Olives, see page 44

Haddock Risotto

Preparation time: 20 minutes
Cooking time: 25 minutes
Serves 4–5

Suggested menu
Haddock Risotto
Cold Meat
Salad
Crumb Trifle *page 78*

1 12 oz. smoked haddock, or fillet smoked fish
2 oz. margarine, or chicken fat
1 onion
6–8 oz. long grain rice
½ pint chicken stock, or water
2 tomatoes

small can peas, or packet frozen peas
seasoning
1 oz. sultanas

to garnish
chopped parsley

Poach the haddock for 5–6 minutes in water (or allow sufficient time for the fish to be removed from the skin; do *not* over-cook). Break the haddock into large flakes, and measure ½ pint fish stock. Heat the margarine, or fat, add the chopped onion and the rice, and turn around in the pan for several minutes. Pour in the fish and chicken stocks, bring to the boil, lower the heat, cover the pan and cook for 10 minutes. Add the skinned chopped tomatoes, peas, fish, seasoning and sultanas; continue cooking in an uncovered pan until the rice is tender and the liquid absorbed. Pile on to a hot dish, and garnish with parsley.

To vary
a) *Kedgeree:* the recipe above is not unlike Kedgeree; but in that recipe you heat 1–2 oz. margarine, add approximately 6–8 oz. *cooked* rice and the same amount of flaked *cooked* haddock, a little milk or thin cream to moisten, and when hot pile on to a hot dish and garnish with chopped hard-boiled egg or eggs, and/or fried onion rings.
b) Use fresh fish instead of smoked haddock.
c) Use shell fish instead of smoked haddock.

Creamed Mussels

Preparation time: 25 minutes
Cooking time: 20 minutes
Serves 8 as an hors d'oeuvre;
4 for a main course

Suggested menu
Melon
Creamed Mussels
Boiled Rice, or boiled noodles
page 54
Green Salad *page 66*
Cheese and biscuits

3 pints mussels
1 onion
½ lemon
seasoning
½ pint water
bouquet garni

for the sauce
1 oz. margarine
1 oz. flour
¼ pint milk
2–3 tablespoons thin cream

to garnish
2 slices bread

Prepare the mussels as page 26, adding the chopped onion and thinly pared lemon rind to the seasoned water; add the *bouquet garni*. Meanwhile make the thick sauce. Lift the mussels from the liquid, remove the shells and 'beards'. Strain the liquid from cooking the mussels into the sauce, and stir well over a low heat until smooth. Add the mussels, juice of the ½ lemon, seasoning to taste, and heat *gently* for a few minutes. Toast the bread, cut into triangles. Spoon the mussel mixture into the dish and garnish with the toast.

Note: if you use bottled mussels, add to the sauce with liquid and enough fish stock to give ½ pint.

Sauces that Blend with Fish

White sauce: (coating consistency) melt 1 oz. margarine in a saucepan, remove from the heat and stir in 1 oz. flour *or* $\frac{1}{2}$ oz. cornflour. Stir over a low heat for several minutes, remove from the cooker once again, gradually blend in $\frac{1}{2}$ pint milk. Bring to the boil, stirring well, cook until thick enough to coat a wooden spoon. Season to taste. A second method of making the sauce is to blend the flour or cornflour *with* the milk, put this into pan with the margarine and seasoning. Bring to the boil gradually, cook as above. Serves 4 in most recipes.

To vary

a) *Anchovy sauce:* make the sauce; be sparing with the salt. Flavour with a few drops of anchovy essence or little paste.

b) *Cheese sauce:* make the sauce, season with salt, pepper *and* mustard. Add 2–4 oz. grated cooking cheese (Cheddar, Cheshire, Dutch, processed, or the more expensive Emmenthal, Gruyère and Parmesan cheese). Heat gently until the cheese melts, do not boil or over-cook, otherwise the sauce could curdle.

c) *Fennel sauce:* make the sauce; add 1 tablespoon finely chopped fennel leaves *or* fennel root.

d) *Horseradish sauce:* make the sauce; add 1–2 teaspoons grated fresh horseradish, or 1 tablespoon horseradish cream.

e) *Lemon sauce:* use fish stock made from bones and skin of fish instead of milk, add the grated rind of a large lemon. Whisk in 1 tablespoon lemon juice to the thickened sauce; simmer gently for 2–3 minutes. Excellent with grilled fish.

f) *Mock Hollandaise sauce:* make the sauce; remove from the heat, whisk in 1 egg yolk beaten with 1 tablespoon vinegar or lemon juice. *Simmer* gently for 2–3 minutes.

g) *Mustard sauce:* blend 1–3 teaspoons dry mustard with the flour, or add made-mustard when sauce has thickened.

h) *Paprika sauce:* blend 1–3 teaspoons paprika with the flour.

i) *Parsley sauce:* make the sauce; add about 1 tablespoon chopped parsley and simmer for 2–3 minutes. Other herbs to use are fresh chives or dill, or try 1 teaspoon only *fresh* oregano, fresh lemon thyme.

Note: (1) for a binding sauce use only $\frac{1}{4}$ pint milk. (2) for a thin (not coating) sauce use 1 pint milk.

Canned concentrated tomato, mushroom, or asparagus soups can be served with fried, or grilled fish, as a sauce.

To make parsley butter

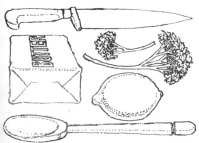

Blend finely chopped parsley and a squeeze lemon juice with butter (or margarine).

Form into a roll, wrap in greaseproof paper and harden in refrigerator. Slice as needed.

Fish Charlotte

Preparation time: 20 minutes
Cooking time: 45 minutes
Serves 4–5

☆☆ **Suggested menu**
Grapefruit, or orange juice
Fish Charlotte
Mashed carrots
Apple Flapjack *page 78*

1 lb. white fish*
seasoning
2–3 tomatoes
4 oz. bread (without crusts)
2 oz. margarine

for the sauce
1 oz. margarine
1 oz. flour
¼ pint milk
1 tablespoon chopped parsley

* use the cheaper fish, such as huss, cod, etc.

Cook the fish in well-seasoned water until just soft. Drain and flake the fish; save ¼ pint of the fish stock. Slice the tomatoes, season lightly. Make the bread into fairly coarse crumbs, see page 43, and toss in the melted margarine. Make the sauce as page 33, add parsley, seasoning, and the fish. Put one-third of the crumbs into a 2-pint casserole or pie dish, then half the tomatoes, and half the fish mixture. Cover with half the remaining crumbs, all the tomatoes and fish mixture, and a final layer of crumbs. Cook for 30 minutes just above the centre of a moderate oven, 375°F., Gas Mark 4–5.

To vary
a) Use a cheese or anchovy sauce instead of parsley sauce.
b) Cut the bread into fingers instead of crumbs; fry in the hot margarine until crisp and brown.
c) *Potato Fish Charlotte:* use layers of firm mashed potato instead of crumbs.

☆☆☆ # Fish Caesar Salad

Preparation time: 15 minutes
Cooking time: 12 minutes
Serves 4–6

☆☆☆ **Suggested menu**
Lemon Soup *page 21*
Fish Caesar Salad
Devilled Potato Salad *page 66*
Gooseberry Creams *page 73*

2 eggs
2 slices bread
1–2 oz. fat, or margarine
lettuce
2–3 tomatoes
small piece cucumber
8–12 oz. cooked white fish, or
canned tuna or pink salmon

2–3 tablespoons salad oil
seasoning
1–1½ tablespoons vinegar
1–2 tablespoons mayonnaise
1–2 oz. Cheddar, or Cheshire
cheese

Boil the eggs for 10 minutes, plunge into cold water to prevent a dark line forming round the yolks. Meanwhile, cut the bread into tiny dice and fry in the hot fat, or margarine, until crisp and brown. Drain for a few minutes on absorbent paper. Wash, drain, and divide lettuce into separate leaves. Put into a salad bowl, top with sliced tomatoes (skin if wished), sliced cucumber, flaked fish, and chopped egg whites. Blend the oil, seasoning and vinegar and spoon over this part of the salad. Top with mayonnaise, the grated or chopped cheese, fried bread and chopped egg yolks.

To vary
a) Add cooked green beans to the lettuce, etc.
b) Top with anchovy fillets as well as cheese, etc.

34

Autumn Fish: arrange 4 portions of uncooked white fish in a greased dish. Beat 1 egg, or 1 egg yolk, with 6 tablespoons milk, 1–2 tablespoons chutney, and seasoning, then add 2 teaspoons grated or chopped onion. Spoon over the fish, and cover the 'sauce' with a layer of crisp breadcrumbs and small pieces of margarine. Bake in the centre of a moderate oven, 375°F., Gas Mark 4–5, for 25–35 minutes, depending upon the thickness of the fish. Extra protein is given by the egg and milk. Serves 4.

Cheese and Haddock Fillets: coat sufficient portions of fresh haddock with milk, or beaten egg, and a mixture of fine *soft* breadcrumbs and grated cheese. Fry in shallow fat for approximately 10 minutes until cooked.

Cheese Topping: to add extra protein (at low cost) to fish, top grilled, baked or fried fish with a thin slice of cheese when the fish is nearly ready. Continue to cook for a few minutes so that the cheese melts and/or browns.

Fish Cakes: these can be made with any fish — white, oily, canned (cooked kippers, tuna and huss, are particularly good). Mix about 8 oz. cooked fish and the same amount of mashed potato (if using instant potato powder make this with *slightly* less water than usual). Bind with an egg, or an egg yolk, and 1 tablespoon milk or water, or with a few tablespoons *very thick* white, anchovy, cheese or parsley sauce (see Note (1), page 33), and season well. Form into about 6–8 small round cakes, coat each with milk, or egg white, or a beaten egg, and breadcrumbs; or, to give a thicker coating, dip in seasoned flour *then* in the milk or egg, etc. Fry in shallow fat until crisp and golden brown. Serves 4.

Fish Rice Cakes: use cooked rice in place of mashed potatoes in the recipe for fish cakes, above; or shape the mixture into *croquettes* (fingers) instead.

Fish Flan: make and bake a 7–8-inch flan case. Blend $\frac{1}{4}$ pint thick anchovy sauce (see Note (1), page 33), with 1 tablespoon chopped cucumber or gherkins, 8–12 oz. flaked cooked or canned fish. Spoon into the flan case, top with 1–2 oz. grated cheese and heat for a short time. Serves 4–6.

Fish in Savoury Custard: arrange 4 small portions of uncooked white fish, or several herring roes, in a greased dish. Beat 1 egg with seasoning, a pinch of mixed herbs, and just under $\frac{1}{2}$ pint warm milk. Pour over the fish, and cover the dish with greased foil. Stand the dish in a container of cold water and bake in the centre of a very moderate oven, 325–350°F., Gas Mark 3–4, for about 35–45 minutes, or until the custard is lightly set and the fish tender. Serves 4.

Seafood Pie: make $\frac{1}{2}$ pint white, anchovy, or cheese sauce. Mix with 12 oz. mixed flaked or chopped fish: use a mixture of white, smoked, and shell fish, if possible. Add 1–2 chopped hard-boiled eggs, and season lightly. Put into a 2-pint pie dish. Top with about 12 oz. mashed potatoes. If all ingredients are hot simply brown under the grill, but if cold heat for 30 minutes in a moderate oven. If fish is scarce, add some chopped cooked bacon or ham to the sauce. Serves 4–5.

Penny-wise Ideas for Fish Dishes

MEAT AND POULTRY

preparation and cooking time

quick ☆☆☆

over ¾ hour but ☆☆
under 2 hours

over 2 hours ☆

Meat and poultry account for a high proportion of the family budget, for it is felt they are essential foods as well as both interesting and sustaining.

The cheaper cuts of meat are equally as nourishing as the prime joints – the steaks, chops, etc. – but they do need more interesting treatment, such as well-spiced gravies, sauces, etc.

Remember if you add beans, peas or lentils, to a stew you can buy less meat or chicken, for these vegetables are good sources of protein. One of the problems facing busy housewives, who may have a full or part-time job, is that stews and casserole dishes take much longer to cook, and have therefore to be planned well ahead. One solution is to cook the stew or casserole one day, allow it to become cold, store it in the refrigerator or a cool place, and then reheat on the second day. Strangely enough the taste is not impaired – in fact the second heating (providing the food was not over-cooked on the first occasion) seems to provide an even better flavour.

When you buy cheaper joints or frozen poultry for roasting, it is advisable to choose a slower method of cooking; the food shrinks less and keeps more moist, see page 37.

Choose meats with a certain amount of fat, this is an indication of flavour; very lean beef, for example, lacks flavour. Chicken and turkey should not be over-fat.

Modern methods of storing food in cold rooms, or refrigerated counters, generally ensure it is fresh; even so, check carefully and see the flesh of meat and poultry are pleasantly moist (not dry); the fat of meat should be firm; the lean bright coloured.

Choosing wisely

If you deal with a butcher, consult him about the 'best buys'. If you buy your meat, etc., from a supermarket, inspect it critically so you learn to differentiate between good and mediocre quality. Avoid meat with large bones and too much fat. Do not buy over-large joints so that you have to 'use up' cold meat continually, but too-small joints are inclined to dry in cooking and have less flavour. Less expensive cuts are:

Beef: choose topside, brisket, aitchbone for roasting. Minute steaks are best value for grilling. Skirt or chuck, blade-bone, fresh or salted brisket, flank for stewing and boiling.

Lamb and mutton: choose breast and best end of neck for roasting; middle or scrag neck for stewing.

Pork and veal: these generally are more expensive meats, but loin chops are best for grilling, and belly of pork cheap for stews. Bacon is always a good buy – streaky rashers, collar and forehock are the most economical.

Poultry: chicken is comparatively cheap, so this book has concentrated on chicken dishes. A turkey can be economical for large numbers.

This method of roasting is ideal for the less tender and, therefore, cheaper joints. I find it better also for frozen or chilled joints of meat, and frozen poultry. The lower temperature also produces less shrinkage in cooking. One difficulty is that you cannot roast potatoes or cook a Yorkshire pudding successfully when the heat of the oven is lower, but the method suggested below will solve the problem.

Slow Roasting

To roast potatoes: choose small potatoes, or halve large ones. Put into boiling salted water and cook steadily for 15 minutes; strain, dry carefully then roll in a little hot fat. Raise the oven temperature to hot, and cook for 20 minutes. If you wish to keep the lower temperature the whole time though try:

Fondant potatoes: roll peeled potatoes in a little hot fat in a roasting tin, pour away any surplus fat after coating the potatoes, then add about 3 tablespoons seasoned water or stock. Cover the tin with foil, for a soft texture, or leave uncovered for a firmer outside, and cook for approximately 1 hour (for medium-sized potatoes) at the heat given below.

Yorkshire pudding: make the batter as page 64. Well grease small patty tins. Raise the temperature of the oven to hot, or very hot if your oven tends to be below average. Heat the tins for 4–5 minutes. Spoon in the batter and cook towards the top of the oven for 15 minutes, or until firm and brown. If wished, remove the meat for most of this time so that it does not become too dry; although the higher temperature gives a pleasing crisp texture.

Times for slow roasting, etc.
Set oven to very moderate 325–350°F., Gas Mark 3–4.

Beef: underdone — 25 minutes per lb. and 25 minutes over. Well done — 35 minutes per lb. and 35 minutes over. Serve with boiled, fondant or roast potatoes, Yorkshire pudding, see above, mustard and/or horseradish sauce or cream, and other vegetables. A thin gravy is usual, see page 52.

Lamb: (normally well done) — 35 minutes per lb. and 35 minutes over. Mutton can be given a few extra minutes per lb. Serve lamb with mint sauce, and mutton with redcurrant jelly or onion sauce, see page 52. Thin gravy usual with lamb; thick with mutton.

Pork: must be well cooked — 35 minutes per lb. and 35 minutes over. Oil the crackling before cooking, and if still not crisping well, raise the oven temperature for the last 20 minutes. Serve with sage and onion stuffing, apple sauce, page 52, and thick gravy.

Veal: must be well cooked — 35 minutes per lb. and 35 minutes over. Accompaniments as for chicken, page 46.

Poultry: see page 46.

All meats — allow extra 30 minutes cooking time when cooking in foil, etc., see page 46.

☆☆☆ Kebabs

Preparation time: 10 minutes
Cooking time: 10 minutes

☆☆☆ **Suggested menu**
Quick Beetroot Bortsch *page 17*
Kebabs
Potato Crisps, or Savoury Rice
page 56
Pain Perdu *page 78*

This method of cooking food under the grill, or over a barbecue fire, needs good quality meat so that it is tender, but it can also prove economical, for the variety of other foods used (vegetables, etc.), 'eke out' the meat in an interesting and sensible manner. It is worthwhile investing in long metal skewers so that you can fit a large enough selection of food on to each skewer. The suggestions below give a variety of kebabs:

a) Put cubes of steak, small parboiled onions, rings of green pepper, sausages or Sausage Savoury Balls (see page 39), small mushrooms, etc., on the skewers.
b) Cut a slice from leg of lamb, dice this, roll in seasoning and a pinch of dried mint, put on skewers with rolls of bacon, tiny tomatoes, small boiled new potatoes, etc.
c) Make Meat Balls with pork (see page 43); put on skewers with rings of dessert apple, dipped in melted butter, or margarine, flavoured with a good pinch of dried sage.

To cook the kebabs: brush lean meat, vegetables, etc., with melted butter, margarine or fat, or Easy Barbecue Sauce (see page 52). Put under the pre-heated grill, cook as quickly as possible until the meat, etc., is tender. Turn several times during cooking. Serve with rice as menu, or vegetables, or fresh rolls and butter, and salad.

To prepare kebabs

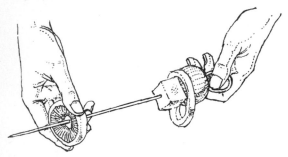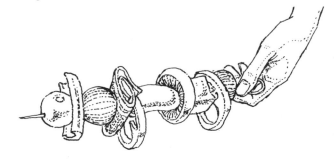

Insert the food on the skewers like this:

☆☆☆ Herbed Steaks

Preparation time: few minutes
Cooking time: 2–4 minutes
Serves 4

☆☆☆ **Suggested menu**
Vegetable Tomato Consommé
page 14
Herbed Steaks
Green Salad
Fresh, canned or frozen fruit
and cream

4 minute steaks (very thin steaks)
seasoning
1 teaspoon chopped mixed
    fresh herbs

2 oz. margarine, butter, or fat

to garnish
watercress

Sprinkle the steaks with seasoning and herbs. Heat the margarine, butter or fat, and fry meat on either side until as cooked as liked; if you want an under-done steak it takes about 1 minute only on either side. Dish up and garnish with watercress.

To vary
Steak au Poivre: omit the herbs, fry the steaks, lift out of pan, and to the fat remaining add $\frac{1}{4}$ teaspoon black pepper or crushed peppercorns, and $\frac{1}{4}$ pint thin or soured cream. Stir over a gentle heat for 2–3 minutes, then pour over the meat.

2 medium onions
1 oz. margarine, or fat
1 lb. sausages

2 dessert apples
½ pint cider
seasoning

Baked Sausages in Cider

Preparation time: 10 minutes
Cooking time: 45 minutes
Serves 4

Peel and slice the onions, and fry in the hot fat in a frying pan for a few minutes. Transfer to an ovenproof dish. Fry the sausages until golden brown. Put into the dish. Core the apples, but do not peel, cut into rings. Arrange round the sausages. Add the cider and seasoning. Cover the dish and cook for about 30–35 minutes in the centre of a moderate oven, 350°–375°F., Gas Mark 4–5.

To vary

a) Use tomato juice in place of cider.
b) Use a can of vegetable soup instead of cider; omit the apples.
c) Use Frankfurter sausages. Heat for about 20 minutes only in the cider.

Suggested menu ☆☆
Baked Sausages in Cider
Bacon Jacket Potatoes *page 41*
Tomato Salad *page 66*
Compôte of Fruit *page 71*

---

1 medium onion
½ small dessert apple
1 oz. margarine
12 oz. sausagemeat
2 oz. soft breadcrumbs
seasoning

to coat
1–2 tablespoons milk
1–2 oz. crisp breadcrumbs

to fry
2 oz. dripping, or fat

Sausage Savoury Balls

Preparation time: few minutes
Cooking time: 10 minutes
Serves 4

Peel and grate the onion and apple, toss in the margarine, then add to the sausagemeat and crumbs, season well. Form into about 12 small balls, brush with milk, roll in crumbs. Heat the fat in a frying pan and cook the balls in this, turning round until they crisp well. Serve hot or cold; or cook as Kebabs, page 38.

To vary

a) *Devilled Sausage Balls:* add ½ teaspoon curry powder, good pinch cayenne pepper, and 1 teaspoon Worcestershire sauce.
b) *Tomato Sausage Balls:* omit the apple, and add 1 teaspoon concentrated tomato purée (bought in tubes or cans) with a good pinch sugar as well as seasoning.
c) *Herbed Sausage Balls:* omit the apple, and add I teaspoon chopped fresh parsley, 1 teaspoon chopped chives, and bind with an egg yolk. Coat in egg white instead of milk, and roll in the crumbs.
d) *Bake* the balls in a moderately hot oven for about 15–20 minutes instead of frying, or cook in a pan of deep fat or oil for 6–7 minutes. Drain on absorbent paper.
e) Use about 4 oz. mashed potato in any of the recipes in place of breadcrumbs.

Suggested menu ☆☆☆
Anchovy Eggs *page 13*
Sausage Savoury Balls
Sauté Potatoes *page 66*
Creamed Spinach *page 66*
Pineapple Condé *page 71*

Corned Beef Hash

Preparation time: 10 minutes
Cooking time: 12 minutes
Serves 4–5

 Suggested menu
Haddock Soup *page 18*
Corned Beef Hash
Sliced Beetroot
Glazed Fruit Fool *page 78*

2 onions
1½–2 oz. dripping, or fat
8–12 oz. corned beef *

8–12 oz. mashed potatoes *
seasoning

* make up to a total of 1¼ lb., if you use 12 oz. corned beef use 8 oz. only of potato.

Peel and chop the onions finely, or grate these. Heat the dripping, or fat, in a large frying pan, and fry the onions for 3–4 minutes. Meanwhile put the corned beef into a basin and flake in small pieces. Add the mashed potatoes, then mix well and season lightly. Spoon into the frying pan and flatten the corned beef mixture. Heat steadily until golden brown on the underside, fold like an omelette and dish-up.

To vary
a) *Tomato Corned Beef Hash:* arrange 2–3 sliced tomatoes over the hash in the pan, heat for a few minutes, then fold.
b) Add a little gravy to the corned beef, etc., to give a softer mixture.

 # Stuffed Marrow

Preparation time: 15 minutes
Cooking time: 25 minutes
Serves 4

Suggested menu
Fresh Cod's Roe Pâté *page 12*
Stuffed Marrow
Potato Nests *page 67*
Fresh Fruit

1 medium marrow
seasoning
1½ oz. margarine

for the stuffing
8–12 oz. cooked meat, or
    corned beef
2 tomatoes

3 oz. soft breadcrumbs
1 teaspoon Worcestershire sauce
good pinch dried herbs
1 egg
seasoning

Peel the marrow, cut into slices approximately 1½–2 inches in thickness. Remove the seeds, season lightly. Put into a steamer and cover with greaseproof paper spread with ½ oz. margarine. Stand over boiling water and steam for 10 minutes only. Mince or chop the meat finely, mix with the skinned chopped tomatoes, 2 oz. crumbs, sauce, herbs, egg and seasoning. Lift the rings of marrow from the steamer. Put into a shallow ovenproof dish. Fill with the stuffing: top with the remainder of the crumbs and the margarine. Bake towards the top of a hot oven, 425–450°F., Gas Mark 6–7, for 15 minutes.

To vary
a) Cut the marrow lengthways, remove the seeds. Put the stuffing into each half. Sandwich together. Wrap in well-greased foil, and bake for 1¼ hours in the centre of a moderate oven. Loosen the foil (so the marrow may brown) and continue cooking for 15–20 minutes.
b) *Rice Stuffed Marrow:* use 3 oz. cooked long grain rice in the stuffing instead of 2 oz. breadcrumbs, and use method a), or the basic method of cooking the vegetables.

1 Vienna loaf
1 oz. margarine
1 bunch spring onions
1 oz. fat
12 oz. corned beef
4 firm ripe tomatoes

seasoning
2 tablespoons mayonnaise, or
    salad dressing
1 teaspoon capers
few lettuce leaves

Viennese Boat

Preparation time: 15 minutes
Cooking time: 10 minutes
Serves 4—5

Suggested menu
Viennese Boat
Mixed Salad or Coleslaw
page 67
Rhubarb Whip *page 72*

Cut a slice from the length of the loaf. Remove most of the crumb; this can be used for a Cheese Charlotte page 64, Fruit Charlotte page 78, or as suggested on page 43. Spread the 'boat shape' left with the softened margarine, and crisp for 8—10 minutes in a hot oven. Chop the spring onions (use two ordinary onions when these are not available) and toss in the hot fat until tender. Add the diced beef, sliced tomatoes, seasoning, mayonnaise, and capers, while the onions are warm. Allow the loaf and the filling to cool. Line the 'boat' with lettuce, and fill with the corned beef mixture. Do not over-handle the filling, as the beef and tomatoes should keep a good shape.

To vary

a) *Rice Vienna Boat:* mix the beef mixture with 2—3 oz. cooked long grain rice. Either heat thoroughly and serve hot, or cool and serve as above.

b) Use minced cooked meat instead of corned beef.

---

4 medium-sized old potatoes
4 streaky bacon rashers, or
    equivalent in bacon pieces

seasoning
2 oz. grated Cheddar cheese

Bacon Jacket Potatoes

Preparation time: 5 minutes
Cooking time: 1¼ or 1½ hours
Serves 4

Suggested menu
Baked Sausages in Cider
page 39
Tomato Salad *page 66*
Bacon Jacket Potatoes
Compôte of Fruit *page 71*

Wash, and prick the potatoes with a fork, so the skin does not break. Bake for approximately 1¼ hours above the centre of a very moderate oven, 325°F., Gas Mark 3, or about 1 hour in a moderate oven, 350—375°F., Gas Mark 4—5. Chop and fry the bacon until crisp. When cooked, halve the potatoes, remove the flesh and mash with seasoning. Add the bacon, and half the cheese. Pile back into the potato skins, top with the rest of the cheese, and return to the oven for 10—15 minutes.

To vary

a) Although given as part of a menu (after the main dish) the above recipe makes an excellent supper dish by itself, or with a salad.

b) Mix the mashed potato with fried chopped onions, flaked corned beef, or minced cooked meat, or poultry (plus tiny pieces of stuffing). Return to the oven, as the recipe above.

c) Omit the bacon and use rather more cheese in the filling.

d) *Jacket Potatoes:* bake the potatoes; when cooked, cut a cross at the top of each potato, and top with a knob of margarine, butter or cream cheese. Use as part of a main dish, see page 9.

Herbed Lamb and Tomato Stew

Preparation time: 10 minutes
Cooking time: 1½ hours
Serves 4

☆☆ **Suggested menu**
Herbed Lamb and Tomato Stew
Savoury Potatoes *page 67*
Macédoine of Vegetables
page 66
Mocha Pudding *page 76*

See picture, *page 23*

8 pieces middle, or scrag end,
  neck of lamb
1 oz. flour
1–2 teaspoons chopped fresh
  herbs*

seasoning
1 oz. fat, or margarine
½ pint water, or white stock
3–4 medium onions
1 lb. tomatoes

* parsley mint, sage, thyme, marjoram.

Trim any excess fat from the meat, and put this fat into a saucepan; heat steadily to extract the dripping, then throw the dried pieces of fat away. Mix the flour with half the herbs and seasoning. Coat the meat with this mixture; add the fat or margarine to the dripping in the pan, and fry the meat steadily on both sides until golden brown. Lift out of the saucepan on to a plate. Pour the stock into the saucepan. Skin and slice the onions, and put into the stock with half the sliced tomatoes (skinned if wished). Arrange the meat on top. Cover the pan and simmer for an hour. Add the rest of the herbs and sliced tomatoes, and continue cooking for a further 10–15 minutes.

Spanish Beef Casserole

Preparation time: 15 minutes
Cooking time: 2¼–2½ hours
Serves 5–6

☆ **Suggested menu**
Spiced Sultana Grapefruit
page 9
Spanish Beef Casserole
Jacket Potatoes *page 41*
Green Vegetable
Caramel Pudding *page 75*

See picture, *page 23*, and cover

2 lb. stewing steak
1 lb. onions
1–2 cloves garlic (optional)
2 oz. fat, or dripping
1½ oz. flour

seasoning
1¼ pints brown stock, or water
  and 2 beef stock cubes
2–4 oz. small mushrooms
1–2 fresh or canned red peppers

Cut the steak into neat pieces; peel, and slice the onions into fairly thick rings. Crush the garlic. Fry the onions and garlic for a few minutes in the hot fat, then lift the onions out on to a plate. Mix the flour with the seasoning; roll the meat in the seasoned flour, and toss in any fat remaining in the pan until golden brown. Add the stock, or water and stock cubes, and bring the liquid to the boil; then simmer for a few minutes until you have a smooth sauce. Transfer to a casserole, cover with a lid, or foil, and cook for 1 hour in the centre of a very moderate oven, 325°F., Gas Mark 3. Add the onions, the whole or sliced mushrooms, and the diced peppers. If using fresh peppers discard the core and seeds. Continue cooking for a further 1–1¼ hours. Serve on a bed of pasta spirals.

To vary
a) Use ¾ pint stock and ½ pint dry cider, or cheap red wine. Use small onions and keep whole.
b) Add small or sliced carrots in place of red peppers and mushrooms.
c) Fry the meat and then the onions. Continue cooking together. The onions become much softer than in the first recipe.
d) Cook in a covered saucepan instead of a covered casserole. The liquid tends to evaporate more, so add an extra ¼ pint. Cook small savoury dumplings (see page 15), in the stew.

42

2 large onions
1–2 cloves garlic
2–3 large tomatoes
2 tablespoons oil
½ pint brown stock
1 lb. minced uncooked beef
seasoning
bouquet garni
good pinch dried marjoram

to garnish
chopped parsley

to serve
6–8 oz. cooked spaghetti, see
    page 54

Minced Beef Provençal ☆☆

Preparation time: 10 minutes
Cooking time: 1¼ hours
Serves 4

Suggested menu ☆☆
Potato Soup *page 20*
Minced Beef Provençal
Sprouts, or other green
vegetable
Banana Fritters *page 70*

See picture, *page 27*

Peel, and chop the onions; crush the cloves of garlic, see page 10. Skin, and chop the tomatoes. Heat the oil in a pan, then toss the vegetables in this for a few minutes. Add the stock, bring to the boil. Put in the beef, heat for a few minutes, then stir well to 'break up' the lumps of meat. Season well, add the herbs. Cover the pan and cook for just over an hour. Stir from time to time as the liquid evaporates. Serve on the pasta, and garnish with chopped parsley. In addition to being an economical meat course served with pasta, this can be used as a filling for pancakes.

To vary

a) *Country Minced Beef:* omit the garlic; add thinly sliced or diced carrots to the meat as it cooks.

b) *Curried Minced Beef:* stir 2–3 teaspoons curry powder and ½ oz. flour into the onions, etc., and cook for several minutes. Follow the recipe above, but add 1–2 oz. sultanas, and 1 tablespoon chutney to the beef. As there is a little thickening in the mixture use just over ½ pint stock.

c) *Meat Balls:* use any of the flavourings suggested in the basic recipe and variations a) and b), but use only ¼ pint liquid, so the mixture becomes very firm. This means you will need to stir well as the sauce thickens. If the mixture is still too soft to roll in balls, either continue cooking in an open pan to evaporate surplus liquid, or add 1–2 oz. soft breadcrumbs. Allow the mixture to cool enough to handle, form into balls, then coat in seasoned flour. Fry in hot fat for a few minutes. If preferred form the balls, but do not coat; poach in beef or chicken stock for a few minutes, then serve. These may be served on top of pasta, or hot or cold.
Vary the meat balls by using minced pork; beef and pork together; lamb, or lamb and pork.

To make soft breadcrumbs

Rub stale bread through a sieve
or against a grater
or put into a liquidiser.

To make crisp breadcrumbs

Put pieces of stale bread or soft crumbs on a baking tray.

Crisp in the oven.
Then roll between sheets of greaseproof paper until fine.

Store in an airtight jar.

Beef and Rice Olives

☆☆

Preparation time: 20 minutes
Cooking time: 1½ hours
Serves 4

☆☆ **Suggested menu**
Beef and Rice Olives
Casserole of Mixed Vegetables
page 66
Fresh Fruit
Cheese Tarts *page 61*

See picture, *page 31*

for the stuffing
3 oz. long grain rice
1 large onion
¼ pint water
seasoning
1 teaspoon capers (optional)
1 oz. margarine
3 teaspoons chopped parsley

for the sauce
1 oz. dripping, or fat
1 oz. flour
¾ pint brown stock, or water
and stock cube
1 tablespoon tomato purée, or
tomato ketchup
4 slices topside beef, cut thinly

Put the rice, peeled and chopped onion, cold water, and seasoning into a saucepan, and bring to the boil. Stir briskly, cover the pan, lower the heat, and allow the liquid to simmer for 15 minutes, by which time the rice should be tender and the liquid evaporated. Add the rest of the stuffing ingredients. While the rice is cooking make the sauce, in the usual way, see page 52. Divide the rice stuffing between the slices of meat, roll firmly and tie with cotton or fine string. Put into a casserole, cover with the sauce, then put on the lid or a layer of foil. Cook in the centre of a moderate oven, 350–375°F., Gas Mark 4–5, for about 1 hour 10 minutes: do not over-cook, as topside can become very dry and hard. Serve with extra savoury rice.

To vary
a) Fill the meat with any other stuffing; sage and onion is particularly good.
b) To make a more interesting dish for a party, add chopped red or green pepper to the rice; use ½ pint stock and ¼ pint cheap red wine in the sauce. Arrange the olives on a bed of diced cooked vegetables, and serve with fried button mushrooms on croûtons of fried bread.

☆☆☆ Hamburgers

Preparation time: 15 minutes
Cooking time: 15 minutes
Serves 4–6

☆☆☆ **Suggested menu**
Hamburgers
Toasted Rolls or Cooked
Spaghetti *page 54*
Peas, or beans
Fresh Fruit

1 large old potato
8 oz. minced good quality
(chuck) stewing steak
1 medium onion
1 oz. soft breadcrumbs, or
rolled oats

1 teaspoon Worcestershire
sauce
1–2 teaspoons chopped parsley
pinch mixed herbs
seasoning
1 oz. dripping, or fat

Peel and grate the potato, mix with all ingredients except the dripping, or fat. Form into 4–6 flat cakes. Fry in hot fat for about 15 minutes, turning carefully, for this particular Hamburger breaks easily.

To vary
a) *Bacon Burgers:* use minced streaky bacon, or bacon pieces, instead of minced meat, or use beef sausagemeat.
b) Grill or bake the Hamburgers if more convenient.

1–1½ lb. potatoes
2 large onions
1–1½ lb. middle, or scrag end,
    neck of lamb

seasoning
½ pint stock
1 oz. margarine, or fat

Lancashire Hot-pot ☆

Preparation time: 25–30 minutes
Cooking time: 2 hours
Serves 4

Peel, and slice the potatoes and onions; cut the meat into neat pieces. Arrange in layers in a deep casserole, beginning and ending with potatoes. Season each layer well and add the stock. Cover the top layer of potatoes with the margarine, or fat, then put a lid on the casserole. Cook for approximately 1½ hours in the centre of a very moderate oven, 325°F., Gas Mark 3. Remove the lid, and cook for a further 30 minutes to crisp the potatoes.

To vary

a) *Irish Stew:* use ingredients above, but slice 1 potato. Put the sliced onions, pieces of meat, and sliced potato into a saucepan, add the stock and season. Simmer for 1 hour, add the whole potatoes, cook for a further 35 minutes. Spoon on to the serving dish, and garnish with chopped parsley.
b) Use diced stewing steak in either the hot-pot or stew, instead of lamb. Cook for about the same time.
c) Use slightly less lamb, or beef, and a thinly sliced kidney or lamb's liver, to give extra flavour.

Suggested menu ☆
Fruit Juice
Lancashire Hot-Pot
Pickled Red Cabbage *see below*
Green Vegetable
Baked Custard *page 78*

To pickle red cabbage

Put layers shredded cabbage and kitchen salt in container. Leave 24 hours.

Prepare spiced vinegar by boiling 1 tablespoon pickling spices with each pint malt vinegar. Strain and *cool*.

Pack well-drained cabbage (rinse under cold tap if wished) in jars. Cover with vinegar.

---

12 oz. short crust pastry, see
    page 77
8 oz. streaky bacon
6 large spring onions
6 eggs
seasoning

to glaze
egg, or milk

Brunch Pies ☆☆

Preparation time: 30 minutes
Cooking time: 25–30 minutes
Serves 6

Roll pastry out thinly, and use just over half to line 6 individual foil dishes or 12 deep patty tins. Cut rind from the bacon, chop rashers finely, put into the pastry cases, add the chopped onion. If using foil dishes, break an egg in each, or beat the eggs and spoon into the small cases, season, top with rounds of pastry. Seal the edges, decorate with pastry 'leaves', glaze with beaten egg, or milk. Bake for 15 minutes in the centre of a moderately hot to hot oven, 400–425°F., Gas Mark 5–6, then lower the heat to moderate for a further 10–15 minutes.

Suggested menu ☆☆
for a picnic:
Brunch Pies
Salad, fresh fruit, cheese and biscuits
for a hot meal:
Brunch Pies
Cooked Vegetables
Junket *page 68*
See picture, *page 51*

Beef Indienne

Preparation time: 20 minutes
Cooking time: 2¼–2½ hours
Serves 4–6

Suggested menu
Beef Indienne
Savoury Rice *page 56*
Carrot Coleslaw *page 67*
Orange Sponge Pudding
page 75

1½ lb. stewing steak
1 oz. flour
½–1 teaspoon ground ginger
1 teaspoon curry powder
1 teaspoon sugar
seasoning

2 oz. fat
2 onions
1 pint beef stock
1 oz. raisins
2 teaspoons sweet chutney

Cut the meat into narrow strips. Blend the flour with the ginger, curry powder, sugar, and seasoning, and roll the meat in this. Heat the fat in a pan and fry the peeled sliced onions for a few minutes, then add the meat and cook for 5–8 minutes until lightly browned. Add the stock, bring to boiling point. Stir well, then add the raisins and chutney. Cover the pan, lower the heat and simmer for 2—2¼ hours until very tender.

To vary
a) Add about 3 oz. soaked prunes to the meat, an hour before serving.
b) Use lamb from middle neck, and cook for 1½ hours only. Reduce the amount of stock to ¾ pint and, since the bones weigh heavily in lamb, increase the amount of meat to 2–2¼ lb.
c) For a more colourful dish add strips of green pepper to the meat, etc., about 30 minutes before serving.
d) To use less meat, add cooked or canned haricot or butter beans towards the end of the cooking time.

Turkey and Chicken

Most people would rather have a roasted turkey than one cooked in any other way. While you can use a hot oven — in which case allow 15 minutes per lb. and 15 minutes over for a bird up to 12 lb. and an additional 12 minutes for every 1 lb. over — the slow method of roasting is particularly good for frozen birds. Always calculate the weight AFTER stuffing. Remember frozen turkeys take about 48 hours to defrost, and frozen chickens about 12 hours, if large.

Slow method of roasting: set oven to very moderate, 325°F., Gas Mark 3. Allow 25–30 minutes per lb. and 25–30 minutes over (very broad-breasted birds need longer time).
Very slow method of roasting: set oven to very slow, 275°F., Gas Mark 1. Allow 1½ hours for the first 1 lb. then 25 minutes per lb. after that.

If using foil or a covered roasting tin, open foil or remove lid for last 1 hour, and allow an extra 30 minutes cooking time.

Serve turkey with bread sauce, thickened gravy, roasted sausages, and bacon rolls. Choose veal and sausagemeat stuffings. *Serve chicken* with the same accompaniments as turkey. Choose the slow, rather than very slow method of roasting, unless cooking an older fowl. If preferred, steam the fowl for half the total cooking time, then roast it.

½ tablespoon powdered
  gelatine
¼ pint chicken stock, or water
  and ½ chicken stock cube
¼ pint thin cream, or top of the
  milk
2 teaspoons chopped spring
  onions, or grated onion

* pieces of skin may be used.

12 oz. cooked chicken*
4–6 oz. lightly cooked beef
1 teaspoon chopped parsley, or
  mixed fresh herbs, or pinch
  dried herbs
seasoning

to garnish
lettuce, tomatoes

Chicken and Beef Cream ☆☆☆

Preparation time: 20 minutes
Cooking time: 2 minutes
Serves 4 as main course;
8 as an hors d'oeuvre.

Soften the gelatine in 2 tablespoons of the cold stock; heat rest of stock and dissolve gelatine. Cool, then add the cream and onion. Allow mixture to *stiffen very slightly*, add finely chopped or minced meats, herbs, and season. Put into an oiled mould, or basin. Allow to set, turn out, garnish with lettuce and tomato slices.

Suggested menu ☆☆☆
Orange and Apple Soup
page 21
Chicken and Beef Cream
Carrots, peas, and mashed
potatoes, or salad
Cheese and biscuits or
Speedy Rolls *page 16*

To vary

a) *Savoury Chicken and Beef Mould:* use brown sauce, or gravy, in place of cream.

b) *Chicken and Ham Cream:* use 8 oz. cooked boiled bacon, or ham, and 8 oz. cooked chicken.

c) *Chicken and Ham Mould:* use 8 oz. cooked ham and 8 oz. cooked chicken and ¼ pint tomato juice, in place of cream. Dissolve ¾ *tablespoon* gelatine in the stock. Proceed as basic recipe, but *with* the chicken, etc., add 1–2 tablespoons cooked peas, and 1 tablespoon sliced cucumber.

1½ oz. butter, or margarine
1½ oz. flour
½ pint chicken stock
¼ pint milk
seasoning
8–10 oz. cooked chicken

6–8 oz. cooked boiled bacon, or
  ham (preferably in one slice)
few cooked peas
2 tablespoons thin cream

Chicken and Ham Supreme ☆☆☆

Preparation time: 20 minutes
Cooking time: 20–25 minutes
Serves 4

Make a sauce of coating consistency, see page 33, with the butter, or margarine, flour, chicken stock and milk. Season lightly. Cut the chicken and ham into neat pieces. Put into the sauce and heat for about 10 minutes. Add the peas, cream, and any extra seasoning required. Serve with the Herbed Rice, page 56.
Note. If keeping hot, transfer to the top of a double saucepan.

Suggested menu ☆☆☆
Melon Cocktail *page 9*
Chicken and Ham Supreme
Herbed Rice *page 56*
Green Vegetable
Coconut Plum Dumplings
page 74

To vary

a) Use about 1 lb. of chicken and only 2 oz. ham.

b) Add 2–4 oz. sliced *cooked* mushrooms instead of, or with, the peas, and garnish with triangles of fried bread.

c) *Chicken à la King:* add cooked or canned corn, and diced de-seeded blanched pepper, to the basic recipe.

47

Chicken Pot Au Feu

☆☆

Preparation time: 20 minutes
Cooking time: See method
Serves 4–5
plus other dishes suggested

☆☆ **Suggested menu**
Chicken Pot au Feu
Mixed Vegetables (see method)
Boiled Rice (optional)
Oranged Bananas *page 70*

large boiling fowl, or chicken,
    about 5½–6 lb. when trussed
giblets
seasoning
bay leaf
bouquet garni * or good pinch
    dried herbs
8 medium onions
8 medium carrots
4 sticks chopped celery
    (optional)

8 medium potatoes

for the sauce
1 oz. margarine
1 oz. flour
¼ pint milk
¼ pint chicken stock (see
    method)
2 tablespoons top of the milk
1 tablespoon chopped parsley

* tie together a sprig of parsley, fresh sage, fresh thyme, and any other fresh herbs, and remove before serving.

This dish is very economical, for if only half the chicken is used to provide a sustaining main meal for 4–5 people, you can make a Rillette from the giblets*, page 10, a Chicken Vegetable Soup for 4–6 people, page 22, Chicken and Ham Supreme, page 47 and a Chicken and Beef Cream or Chicken and Ham Mould, page 47. And with the extra stock, Clear Chicken Consommé, page 22.

The amount of vegetables given will vary according to personal taste. Put the chicken into a large saucepan, cover with cold water. Add the giblets, but check that the liver has no green marks from the gall bladder which could make the stock bitter. Bring the water just to the boil, remove any grey sediment, then add seasoning and herbs. Lower the heat *and simmer very gently*. Allow 40 minutes per lb. for a boiling fowl, 30 minutes per lb. for a fairly old chicken, but only 25 minutes per lb. for a young roasting bird. Add the vegetables about ¾–1 hour before serving. Make the sauce: melt the margarine in a pan, then stir in the flour. Cook for several minutes, then remove the pan from the heat and stir in the cold milk. Remove ¼ pint stock from the saucepan. Add this to the sauce. Bring to the boil, stir all the time, and cook until thickened. Add the cream, any seasoning required, and the parsley. To serve, lift bird from pan, slice required amount of chicken on to a dish, coat with the sauce. Arrange a border of cooked rice round the chicken. Serve most of the vegetables in a separate dish, but keep 2 carrots, 2 onions, 2 potatoes and a little celery for the soup.

*Note. If making Rillette of Chicken, remove giblets from stock after one hour's cooking, or when *just* tender. If left longer they lose both flavour and texture.

To vary
The flavour may be altered according to the sauce served:
a) Blend 1–2 teaspoons curry powder with the flour.
b) Add a sliced lemon to the stock when cooking the chicken, and use ½ pint of this, plus 2 tablespoons thick cream; omit the milk. Flavour sauce with 1 teaspoon grated lemon rind.

4 joints frying chicken*
seasoning
1 tablespoon flour
1 oz. butter, or chicken fat

2 tablespoons oil
2 oz. almonds

to garnish
watercress

* when frying chicken I find it better to allow the frozen chicken joints to defrost completely, then dry them well.

Chicken and Almonds ☆☆☆

Preparation time: few minutes*
Cooking time: 15 minutes
Serves 4

Coat the chicken with well-seasoned flour. Heat the butter, or fat, and oil in a large frying pan. Fry the chicken quickly, turning once or twice, until golden brown. Lower the heat so the joints are thoroughly cooked. Blanch the almonds in boiling water, see page 50, and dry well. Lift the chicken from the pan and keep hot; fry the almonds in the pan until golden brown. Spoon over the chicken; garnish with watercress.

Suggested menu ☆☆☆
Curried Cucumber Soup
page 16
Chicken and Almonds
Savoury Rice *page 56*
Broccoli
Ice Cream Sundae *page 78*

To vary

a) *Paprika Chicken:* cook the chicken as above (but omit the almonds). Lift out of the pan when cooked, and keep hot. Blend $\frac{1}{4}$ pint soured cream, or fresh thin cream and $\frac{1}{2}$ tablespoon lemon juice, with 1–2 teaspoons paprika pepper. Heat for a few minutes then spoon the cream mixture over the chicken and garnish with chopped parsley.

b) *Trout and Almonds:* fry fresh (not smoked) trout in the same way as the recipe above. Frozen trout does not need defrosting before cooking.

8–10 oz. cooked chicken
2 oz. mushrooms (optional)
2 tomatoes
2 pickled cucumbers, or
    piece fresh cucumber and
    1 teaspoon vinegar

2 teaspoons capers
2 hard-boiled eggs
3 tablespoons mayonnaise
$\frac{1}{2}$ teaspoon paprika pepper
1 lettuce

Polish Chicken Salad ☆☆☆

Preparation time: 15 minutes
Cooking time: none
Serves 4

Dice the chicken, peel the raw mushrooms, or if very perfect do not peel, just wash thoroughly and slice neatly. Skin and slice the tomatoes, and slices the cucumber thinly. If using fresh cucumber, slice, and leave in the vinegar for 5 minutes. Mix the chicken, mushrooms, tomatoes and cucumber with the capers, the chopped egg whites, mayonnaise and paprika. Pile on to a bed of lettuce and garnish with the chopped yolks of the eggs.

Suggested menu ☆☆
Curried Vegetable Soup *page 17*
Speedy Rolls *page 16*
Polish Chicken Salad
Apple Puffs *page 69*

To vary

a) *Chicken and Apple Salad:* core 2 dessert apples but do not peel. Cut into thin slices, dip in French dressing, see page 52. Arrange on the bed of lettuce, then top with the salad mixture above.

b) *Chicken and Potato Salad:* omit mushrooms and add 4–6 oz. diced potatoes instead.

☆

Creamed Tripe

Preparation time: 15 minutes
plus 1 hour soaking
Cooking time: 1¼ hours
Serves 4

☆ **Suggested menu**
Anchovy Eggs *page 13*
Creamed Tripe
Mashed potatoes and
Macédoine of Vegetables
page 66
Lemon Sponge Pudding
page 75

1–1½ lb. dressed tripe
2 onions
seasoning
1 oz. flour
½ pint milk

1 oz. margarine

to garnish
chopped parsley

Tripe is one of the most economical of meats and is more versatile than people imagine

Cut the tripe into neat strips. Soak for 1 hour in cold water, then put into a saucepan in fresh cold water. Bring the water to the boil and strain the tripe. This process, called blanching, both whitens the tripe and gives a better flavour. Put the tripe back into a pan with the sliced onions, a generous ½ pint water, and seasoning. Simmer in a covered pan for 1 hour. At the end of this time the water in the pan should have evaporated to give about ¼ pint. Blend the flour with the milk, stir into the tripe mixture, add the margarine and cook, stirring well, until a smooth thickened sauce. Season again, Spoon into the serving dish, and top with chopped parsley.

To vary
a) *Tripe Mornay:* cook the tripe with the onions as above. Make ½ pint Cheese sauce, page 33, and blend with the tripe and onions. Put into a heatproof dish, top with breadcrumbs and grated cheese and brown under the grill.
b) *Farmhouse Tripe:* cook the tripe and onions as above, but add 2–3 sliced carrots and 1 small sliced turnip. When the tripe is cooked, blend 1 oz. flour with ¼ pint brown stock, instead of milk. Add to the tripe, etc., with 1 oz. dripping, or margarine, and cook until thickened.
c) *Stuffed Tripe:* do not cut the tripe into strips, but keep in one whole piece. Wash and blanch as above, then spread with sage and onion stuffing, see page 52. Roll firmly, and put into a casserole. Cover with 1 pint brown sauce, foil or a casserole lid, and cook for 1½ hours in the centre of a very moderate oven, 300–325°F., Gas Mark 2–3.

To blanch almonds

Put boiling water into a basin, add the nuts – or drop nuts into the pan, but DO NOT continue heating.

Leave for 1–2 minutes only, so they do not become too soft. Lift out and remove skins.

Brunch Pies, see page 4

Stuffings and Sauces

Stuffings add interest to many dishes, they also help to keep meat and poultry moist, and make a more substantial meal. The quantities of stuffings and sauces are enough for 4–6 people.

Apple and Celery stuffing: for meats. Peel and dice 4 oz. cooking apples, mix with equal quantities of soft crumbs, chopped celery, seasoning, 1 tablespoon chopped parsley, 2 teaspoons brown sugar. Bind with 1 egg or a little stock.

Rice stuffing: for poultry, meats, vegetables, fish. Boil 3 oz. long grain rice, blend with 1 oz. margarine, 2 tablespoons chopped parsley, 1 oz. sultanas, 1 large grated onion. Bind with stock, milk or an egg, season well.

Sage and Onion stuffing: for pork, etc. Peel and chop 2 large onions, simmer in a little salted water until nearly tender, strain. Blend onions with 2 oz. soft crumbs, 1 teaspoon dried and 2 teaspoons fresh chopped sage, seasoning, 1–2 oz. shredded suet, or melted margarine, and onion stock to bind.

Sausagemeat stuffing: for meats, poultry, etc. Blend 1 lb. sausagemeat with 2 rashers streaky bacon, chopped finely, and 2 oz. soft crumbs. Add herbs to taste, and a little milk or egg. Add a few sultanas, or chopped nuts, or celery if wished.

Veal (Parsley and Thyme) stuffing: for poultry, fish, veal, etc. Blend 4 oz. soft crumbs with 1–2 oz. shredded suet, $\frac{1}{2}$ teaspoon dried or 1 teaspoon fresh chopped mixed herbs, $\frac{1}{2}$–1 tablespoon chopped parsley. Bind with stock, milk, or an egg.

Cook stuffings in the poultry, or in a 'pocket' in meat. Or allow about 1 hour in a moderate oven, in a covered container.

A good sauce can turn a plain dish into an interesting one.

Apple sauce: for pork, etc. Simmer 1 lb. peeled, sliced cooking apples in $\frac{1}{4}$ pint water, add sugar to taste. Beat or sieve.

Bread sauce: for poultry, veal, etc. Infuse 1 onion in $\frac{1}{2}$ pint milk, add 2 cloves if wished. Stir in $\frac{1}{2}$–1 oz. margarine and 2 oz. soft white crumbs, heat gently and remove onion.

Brown sauce: for savoury dishes. Make as White sauce, page 33, but use brown stock instead of milk and dripping, or fat, instead of margarine. Flavour with chopped onion if wished.

Easy Barbecue sauce: add 1–2 tablespoons tomato ketchup, 1 tablespoon Worcestershire sauce, 2 teaspoons mustard, to above.

French dressing: for salads. Blend 4 tablespoons oil, 2 tablespoons lemon juice, or vinegar, seasoning and pinch sugar.

Gravy: for all meats. Pour away all fat from cooking meat except 1 tablespoon; retain the meat residue. Blend 1–2 level tablespoons flour (according to thickness required) into the fat, cook for several minutes then blend in about $\frac{3}{4}$ pint stock and gravy browning. Cook well and strain.

Horseradish sauce: blend horseradish cream, or grated horseradish to taste, into White sauce, see page 33, or thick cream.

Onion sauce: add chopped cooked onion to White or Brown sauce.

Tartare sauce: for fish, etc. Blend chopped parsley, gherkins and capers to taste, into salad dressing or mayonnaise.

Chicken Pudding: remove the meat from the bones of a small boiling fowl; use the bones for stock, and use in soups, etc. Dice the meat and continue as Meat pudding, below. Serves 4–6.

Meat Pudding: make a suet crust with 8 oz. self-raising flour, pinch salt, 3–4 oz. shredded suet and water to bind. Roll out thinly, line a $1\frac{1}{2}$–2-pint basin with about two-thirds of dough. Fill with 1 lb. well-seasoned diced, or minced, stewing steak, 2–3 thinly sliced onions, 2–3 sliced tomatoes, and $\frac{1}{4}$ pint stock. Cover with the remaining suet crust pastry rolled into a round, then with greased paper, or foil. Steam over boiling water for about 3 hours if using minced beef, or 4 hours if using diced meat. If you use less meat, add 2–3 oz. soaked and *cooked* dried haricot or butter beans, or peas, to the filling. Serves 4–6.

Dumplings: traditionally dumplings were served BEFORE the main course, so that the family felt well satisfied and ate less of the more expensive meat, etc. If you 'revive' this old custom, make dumplings as page 15, but use 4 oz. flour, etc. for 4–6 people. Boil the balls in stock, or well-seasoned boiling water, for about 20 minutes; serve topped with grated cheese, or with a brown gravy. The dumplings may be added to any stew, or to boiled chicken, see page 48; make sure you have plenty of liquid before putting them into the pan.

Durham Cutlets: make a thick white or brown sauce with 1 oz. margarine or fat, 1 oz. flour, $\frac{1}{4}$ pint milk or stock. Add 8 oz. raw minced beef, 4 oz. soft breadcrumbs, a good pinch mixed herbs. Form into cutlet shapes and coat in milk or egg and crumbs. Fry *steadily* until crisp and golden brown. To vary the flavour, add a chopped onion to the fat and fry gently before making the sauce. If preferred the cutlets may be baked on a well-greased tin for about 45 minutes in the centre of a moderate oven. Serves 4.

Rissoles: these are made as the Durham cutlets above, but use cooked, minced or finely chopped, meat or chicken instead of raw meat. Since this will be drier, reduce the amount of crumbs to 2 oz. Fry fairly quickly, or bake for about 25 minutes only, since the meat is spoiled by reheating for too long a period. Serves 4.

Viennese Steaks: this is a good way to use minced beef to form into a substitute for steak. Mix 1 lb. minced beef with 1 tablespoon tomato ketchup, or 2 teaspoons concentrated tomato purée, 2 teaspoons chopped parsley, little grated nutmeg and seasoning. Bind with 1 egg yolk or a very little stock. Form into 4–6 round shapes with well-floured hands. Fry in hot fat until brown on either side (turn carefully since it is a mixture that breaks easily), then lower the heat and cook steadily for about 5 minutes. Serve with rings of onion, dipped in egg white, then flour, and fried until crisp and golden brown. Serves 4–6.

To vary
a) Add a pinch of curry powder.
b) Omit the tomato flavouring and add Worcestershire sauce, or add a generous amount of black pepper.

PASTA AND RICE

preparation and cooking time

quick ☆☆☆

over ¾ hour but ☆☆
under 2 hours

over 2 hours ☆

These two foods are excellent in providing the basis of economical meals. They combine well with all savoury ingredients; some pasta (macaroni in particular) can be used in sweet dishes, see page 57, and rice is one of the most versatile ingredients in puddings.

Use cooked pasta and rice *with* main dishes, as a change from potatoes. Never waste these foods; if any are left, cover and store in a cool place. Reheat by putting into lightly salted *cold* water. Bring to the boil as quickly as possible, strain and use.

To cook pasta: follow the directions for quantity of water as given below. Do not over-cook; all pasta should be slightly firm when tested with a fork.

To cook rice: this depends upon the particular dish, but the simplest method of boiling rice is as described in the recipe for Herbed Rice, page 56, i.e. to put the rice into *cold* liquid, bring to the boil, etc. Naturally you will use salted water, not stock, for plain boiled rice, and about twice as much water as rice, i.e. 1 cup rice — 2 cups water; 1 oz. rice — 2 fluid oz. water. This means there is no need to strain or rinse the rice.

To cook spaghetti

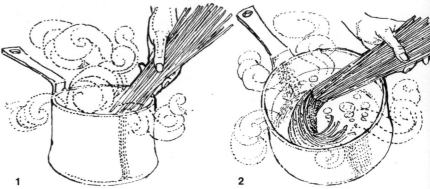

1
To each 4 oz. pasta allow minimum 2 pints water. Bring to boil, add salt to taste. Lower ends of spaghetti into this, hold rest of pasta.

2
Boil for about 2 minutes, until the ends begin to soften. Twist the pasta, so more is covered with the water.

3
Continue like this until all the pasta is in the water. Boil rapidly.

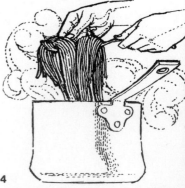

4
Lift once or twice with two forks to separate the strands. Cook until just tender. Strain and serve.

54

Macaroni Cheese, see page 57

Herbed Rice

Preparation time: 5 minutes
Cooking time: 20 minutes
Serves 4–5

  Suggested menu
Melon Cocktail *page 9*
Chicken and Ham Supreme
page 47
Herbed Rice
Green Vegetable
Coconut Plum Dumplings
page 74

¾ pint chicken stock
4 oz. long grain rice

seasoning
1 tablespoon chopped fresh herbs*

* parsley, thyme, mint, sage.

Put chicken stock and rice into a pan. Season well. Bring the stock to the boil, stir briskly. Cover the pan, lower the heat, cook gently for 15 minutes: the rice should then be tender and stock absorbed (if not, cook for a few minutes with the lid removed). Add the herbs; stir well and serve.

To vary
a) Use water in place of stock.
b) *Saffron Rice:* blend a good pinch of saffron powder with water, or stock, or infuse about 10–12 strands of saffron in the water, or stock, for about 1 hour, strain the liquid (which will have absorbed both colour and flavour) and cook as recipe.
c) *Fruit Rice:* cook as Herbed Rice; add 2 oz. raisins, 4 tablespoons chopped canned pineapple, 1–2 tablespoons chopped green pepper, heat for about 2 minutes; omit herbs, if wished.

Savoury Rice

Preparation time: 5 minutes
Cooking time: 25 minutes
Serves 4–6

  Suggested menu
Beef Indienne *page 46*
Savoury Rice
Carrot Coleslaw *page 67*
Orange Sponge Pudding
page 75

1 oz. fat, or margarine
1 onion
6 oz. long grain rice
½ pint water

seasoning
1 carrot
1 oz. raisins
½–1 tablespoon chopped parsley

Heat the fat, or margarine, and fry the peeled sliced onion for a few minutes, then add the rice. Stir well, and turn in the fat and onion for 1 minute, then add the water and seasoning. Bring to the boil in an uncovered pan, then stir again. Put on the lid and simmer for nearly 15 minutes, when the rice should be almost soft. Add the coarsely grated carrot, and raisins, and mix with the rice. Continue cooking for a few more minutes until the rice is tender (do not over-cook) and the liquid evaporated. Top with parsley.

To vary
a) Stir 1–2 teaspoons curry powder into the onion and fat.
b) Add cooked peas, carrots or any other cooked vegetables, to the rice when it is *nearly* cooked, or add grated or diced raw vegetables when the water is boiling.
c) Add diced cooked ham, or other meat, or flaked cooked or canned fish, or diced hard-boiled eggs to basic recipe or a) or b). This makes a good hors d'oeuvre, enough for 8–9 people.
d) Add tiny pieces of well-drained canned pineapple, and chopped raw green pepper, to basic recipe just before serving.

Note. Toss any variation in a little mayonnaise, or oil and vinegar, allow to cool, and serve cold as a salad.

Penny-wise Ideas for Pasta and Rice

Macaroni Cheese: cook 3–4 oz. short length macaroni until just tender, in boiling salted water. Strain, but if you wish to economise on milk in the sauce, save a little of the macaroni liquid. While the macaroni is cooking prepare the sauce – if you are putting hot macaroni into hot sauce and browning the dish under the grill, make a cheese sauce, as page 33, with 1½ oz. margarine, 1½ oz. flour, ¾ pint milk, or milk and macaroni water, seasoning, and 4 oz. grated cheese. If you intend to allow the dish to stand, to be reheated later in the oven, use only 1 oz. margarine and 1 oz. flour to the ¾ pint liquid, etc. Mix the macaroni with the sauce, put into an ovenproof dish, or flameproof dish if you intend to brown this under the grill. Top with grated cheese and a few crumbs. Brown under a moderately hot grill, or heat for 30 minutes in a moderate oven. Serves 4–5.
Small pieces of cooked chicken, ham, or bacon could be added. Garnish with tomatoes, parsley and crisp bacon, if wished. See picture, page 55.

Macaroni Custard: this can be sweet or savoury. Boil 3 oz. short length macaroni until nearly tender, in lightly salted boiling water; drain well. Beat 2 eggs, add 1 pint milk, and either seasoning or 1–2 oz. sugar. Mix with the macaroni and put into a pie dish. Top with grated cheese or with grated nutmeg, if wished. Bake for about 1 hour in the centre of a slow oven until set. Serves 4–5.
If you wish to economise on eggs, blend 1 level tablespoon cornflour with milk, cook until slightly thickened, pour over 1 beaten egg, add the macaroni, etc., cook as above.

Speedy Spaghetti Milanaise: cook spaghetti as page 54, strain. Heat a can of condensed tomato soup, serve as a sauce over the pasta. Top with grated cheese and parsley.
Other soups to use are mushroom, mulligatawny, chicken: if using thinner soups, thicken with a teaspoon of cornflour.

Pasta Marinara: cook 4–6 oz. any pasta, strain and tip back in the pan with a knob of margarine, a small can tuna fish and plenty of seasoning, including garlic salt. Heat well, then pile on to a hot dish, and top with cooked tomatoes or tomato soup. A more definite flavour is given if a few chopped anchovies are added to the pasta, and tuna and extra anchovies arranged on top before serving. If wished, you can fry chopped onions, mushrooms and tomatoes, and mix these with the pasta and tuna. Serves 4–6.

Rice or Pasta Omelettes etc.: add 1–2 oz. cooked rice, or cooked chopped pasta to 3–4 beaten eggs for an omelette. Fry 2 rashers chopped bacon in a pan, with a chopped onion, add ½ oz. margarine and 1–2 oz. cooked rice, or chopped cooked pasta. Heat thoroughly, then add 3 beaten seasoned eggs, and scramble in the usual way. Serves 3–4.

Curried Rice: fry 2 chopped onions in 1 oz. margarine, add 1–2 teaspoons curry powder and ¼ pint stock. Heat thoroughly, then add 4–6 oz. cooked long grain rice, about 8 oz. cooked diced meat, or flaked fish, a few sultanas. Heat gently and serve with chutney. Serves 3–4.

Round rice (for puddings)

Long grain rice

EGG AND CHEESE DISHES

preparation and cooking time

quick ☆☆☆

over ¾ hour but ☆☆
under 2 hours

over 2 hours ☆

Few foods are so versatile as an egg; it is an essential ingredient in most cakes; the basis of many puddings, as well as savoury dishes. In this section are some easy egg dishes that can be served for main meals in place of meat or fish.

Pancakes, omelettes, and baked eggs are ideal ways of combining eggs with small quantities of meat, or fish, or vegetables. Although most egg dishes should be served immediately after cooking (so they do not dry), pancakes, plus the fillings, may be prepared in advance, if more convenient. Cook the pancakes and separate them with squares of greaseproof paper. Wrap the pile of pancakes in greaseproof paper, or foil; store in a cool place, or the refrigerator, or home freezer, and 'peel off' as many as are required, see page 64.

Never waste cheese by poor storage. Keep it well-wrapped in the refrigerator, or larder, so it does not become dry and hard. If pieces of cheese *do* become stale, then grate or chop finely, and use as an ingredient in sandwiches, salads, or, if the type that cooks well, in sauces and savoury dishes.

Children should be encouraged to eat cheese as often as possible for it is rich in calcium, which is essential for healthy teeth and bones, as well as protein. There is no easier or quicker light meal than bread or biscuits, cheese, butter, salad and/or fruit. Cheese is easily spoiled by over-cooking. A cheese sauce that is cooked for too long a period will curdle; a cheese topping becomes 'stringy'.

Both cheese and egg dishes are ideal for high tea or supper, for they are satisfying yet not too 'stodgy'.

Choosing wisely

Buy smaller-sized eggs (which are less expensive), for cooking, or for small children who may not require a large egg. Occasionally you may see cracked eggs at reduced prices – providing these are *very fresh*, they are satisfactory for cooking.

Most grocers and supermarkets have a large selection of cheeses. Do not buy too large a range at one time, unless you are having a party, for some could be wasted. Undoubtedly the best cheese to buy is Cheddar, for it an excellent cooking cheese as well as being the most popular to eat uncooked. Other less expensive (and versatile) cheeses are: Cheshire, Lancashire, Dutch Edam and Gouda, Danish Blue, cottage and processed.

Pasta and savoury rice dishes such as risotto are both filling and economical, and are given extra flavour with a cheese topping. Italian recipes generally suggest Gruyère or Parmesan, but both of these are fairly costly, so choose Cheddar or Cheshire as cheaper alternatives.

If you wish to make creamed potatoes more interesting, add a beaten egg and/or grated cheese just before serving.

Apple and Raspberry Cobbler, see page 69

To make Omelettes

Omelettes are some of the most appetising egg dishes, and they can be served at any meal. For adults, allow a minimum of 2 eggs per person or 3 eggs between 2 people; for small children you can make the omelette serve a larger number.

Butter is generally used to cook an omelette, for it adds flavour and helps to prevent the omelette sticking to the pan. It is wise to invest in a special small pan for cooking omelettes and pancakes. Wipe — do not wash — after use.

To make an omelette for 1 person: heat about $\frac{1}{2}$–1 oz. butter (or use oil or clarified fat) in a 5–6-inch pan. Beat 2 eggs with seasoning and $\frac{1}{2}$ tablespoon water. Pour into the hot butter and allow the mixture to cook for about 30 seconds. At the end of this time the eggs will have set in a thin layer at the bottom, so you now begin to 'work' the omelette. To do this tilt the pan; at the same time loosen the eggs away from the edge so the liquid egg from the top runs to the edge and bottom, and begins to set. As soon as the eggs are as set as you would wish, fold the omelette away from the handle, tip on to a hot plate, and serve at once.

Flavour omelettes: by adding mixed herbs to the eggs.
Fill omelettes before folding: with grated cheese; cooked vegetables; sliced raw tomatoes; left over cooked fish, or meat.
Make the eggs go further: blend 2 eggs with 2 tablespoons *smooth* mashed potato; with 2 tablespoons fine soft crumbs: cook as above, or fry croûtons of bread *first*, then mix with eggs.

☆☆

Potato Soufflé

Preparation time: 5 or 15 minutes
Cooking time: 50 or 30 minutes
Serves 4

☆☆   **Suggested menus**
for high tea or supper:
Cheese Tomato Charlotte *page 64*
Potato Soufflé
Green or Mixed Salad
Banana and Apple Jelly *page 72*

for lunch or dinner:
Orange and Grapefruit
Cocktail *page 13*
Potato Soufflé
Salad or spinach
Banana and Apple Jelly *page 72*

Also an excellent
accompaniment to cold meats,
cheese, egg, or fish dishes.

1 lb. old potatoes, or medium packet dehydrated (instant) potatoes
1 oz. margarine
4 tablespoons milk
2 eggs
seasoning

Peel, and cook potatoes until tender, then mash, or reconstitute potatoes according to instructions on packet. Add margarine, milk, egg yolks, then season well. Fold in the stiffly beaten egg whites. Spoon into a 7-inch soufflé or ovenproof dish. Bake towards the top of a moderately hot to hot oven for approximately 25 minutes, until well risen. Serve at once.

To vary
a) *Cheese Potato Soufflé:* add 3 oz. grated cheese to the mashed potatoes, before the egg yolks, etc.
b) *Fish Potato Soufflé:* add 4 oz. flaked, cooked or canned, fish before the egg yolks, etc.
c) *Ham Potato Soufflé:* add 3–4 oz. finely chopped or minced cooked ham, or boiled bacon, before the egg yolks, etc.
Note. The Potato Soufflé, with the addition of the eggs, is an excellent way to supplement the protein in a meal.
Each variation makes a complete light supper dish.

1 lb. prepared potatoes
seasoning
2 large carrots
2 large onions

for the topping
2 oz. grated Cheddar cheese

for the sauce
1 oz. margarine
1 oz. flour
$\frac{1}{4}$ pint milk
2 oz. grated Cheddar cheese

Farmhouse ☆☆
Pie

Preparation time: 30 minutes
Cooking time: 1 hour
Serves 4

Suggested menu　　　☆☆
Sardine Salad *page 11*
Farmhouse Pie
Brussels sprouts, or other
green vegetable
Date and Apple Crisp *page 76*

Cook the potatoes in boiling salted water until soft, but unbroken. Strain, and cool enough to handle. Peel the carrots and onions, chop fairly coarsely and cook in boiling, well-seasoned water until soft. Strain, and retain $\frac{1}{4}$ pint of the stock. Make a sauce with the margarine, flour, milk and vegetable stock. Season lightly. Add the cheese, the chopped carrots and onions, and put into a 2-pint pie dish. Cover with the sliced potatoes and the rest of the cheese. Heat for about 25 minutes towards the top of a moderate oven, 350–375°F., Gas Mark 4–5, until the topping is brown.

To vary
a) Use a mixture of cooked vegetables in the sauce.
b) Add small pieces of cooked ham, or fried bacon, to the sauce.
c) Top with mashed potatoes and cheese, instead of sliced potatoes and cheese; or with 6 oz. cheese pastry, see page 77.

5–6 oz. short crust pastry
4 oz. cream cheese, or finely
　　grated Cheddar cheese and
　　1$\frac{1}{2}$ tablespoons thin cream

3 eggs
seasoning
2 teaspoons chopped chives, or
　　parsley

Cheese ☆☆☆
Tarts

Preparation time: 25 minutes
Cooking time: 20 minutes
Makes 12

Suggested menu　　　☆☆☆
Beef and Rice Olives *page 44*
Casserole of Mixed Vegetables
page 66
Fresh Fruit, Cheese Tarts

Roll out the pastry and line 12 fairly deep patty tins. Put the cream cheese, or Cheddar cheese and cream, into a basin. Gradually blend in the eggs, seasoning and herbs. Spoon the filling into the tartlet cases. Bake in the centre of the oven for about 10 minutes at 425°F., Gas Mark 6–7, then lower the heat from hot to moderate, 350–375°F., Gas Mark 4–5, and leave for a further 10 minutes, or until the pastry is crisp and the filling set. Serve hot or cold.
Note. These tartlets can be prepared before a meal, then put into the oven when serving the first course. If you do not wish to adjust the heat in baking (as above), then bake for about 25 minutes in a moderate to moderately hot oven.

To vary
a) Add 4 oz. very finely chopped cooked ham to eggs, and omit cheese. Flavour with chopped chives, or spring onions.
b) Blend the eggs with 4 oz. boned mashed pink salmon, and flavour with a little lemon juice as well as seasoning and parsley: omit the cheese or use 1 oz. only.
c) Bake pastry 'blind' as next recipe, add filling and set for 30 minutes in a very moderate oven.

Cheese and Vegetable Flan

☆☆

Preparation time: 30 minutes
Cooking time: 1 hour —
1 hour 10 minutes
Serves 4—6

☆☆ **Suggested menu**
Tomato Lentil Soup *page 18*
Cheese and Vegetable Flan
Duchesse Potatoes *page 67*
Green Salad
Stuffed Baked Apples *page 78*

6 oz. short crust pastry, page 77
2 oz. mushrooms
1 large onion
1 oz. margarine

2—3 tablespoons cooked peas
2 egg yolks, or small eggs
seasoning
½ pint milk (see method)
4 oz. grated Cheddar cheese

Make the pastry as page 77. Roll out, and line a 7—8-inch flan ring on an upturned baking tin or sheet (this makes it easier to remove), or a shallow overproof dish. Bake 'blind', as page 77, for 20 minutes only, in the centre of a hot oven, 400°F., Gas Mark 5—6, until set and pale golden brown. Meanwhile wash and slice the mushrooms and chop the onion finely, then toss in the hot margarine for about 5 minutes. Mix with the peas and put at the bottom of the flan. Beat the egg yolks with seasoning, add the warmed milk. If the dish is very shallow use just under the ½ pint milk. Add the grated cheese, and pour into the pastry case. Lower the oven heat to very moderate, 325—350°F., Gas Mark 3—4, and bake in the centre of the oven for a further 40 minutes, or until the filling is firm to the touch. Serve hot or cold.

To vary
a) Use a mixture of about 6 oz. diced cooked vegetables; it is perhaps wise to avoid using tomatoes, since they can cause the egg and milk mixture to curdle; but you can top the flan with 2—3 skinned sliced tomatoes about 10 minutes before the end of the cooking time. Return the flan to the oven to complete cooking.
b) *Quiche Lorraine:* omit vegetables and add about 4—6 oz. crisply fried chopped bacon instead.
c) *Onion and Potato Flan:* use about 6 oz. diced, or thinly sliced, cooked new or old potatoes, and 1—2 sliced onions, fried in 1 oz. margarine. Omit bacon or other vegetables.

Cheeseolettes

☆☆☆

Preparation time: 5 minutes
Cooking time: 10 minutes
Makes 8—10

☆☆☆ **Suggested menu**
Tomato Salad *page 66*
Cheeseolettes
Rolls and butter
Fresh Fruit or ice cream and canned fruit

2 eggs
2 oz. self-raising flour (or plain flour and ½ teaspoon baking powder)
2 oz. grated cheese

seasoning
2 oz. fat

to garnish
parsley

Beat all the ingredients, except fat and parsley, together. Heat the fat in a large pan, drop in spoonfuls of the mixture. Do not put too many in the pan at one time, as these fritters are fairly fragile and need care in turning. Cook for 1½—2 minutes over a steady heat, turn and cook for the same time on the second side. Lift out, there is no need to drain on paper. Fry the next batch, and continue like this. Serve hot or cold, garnished with parsley. These should be eaten when fresh. You can flavour the mixture with herbs, curry powder, etc.

Gypsy Tart, Lemon Soufflé and Chocolate/lime Ice Cream Sundae, see pages 77, 73 and 78

Cheese Tomato Charlotte

Preparation time: 10–15 minutes
Cooking time: 35–40 minutes
Serves 4

 Suggested menus
for high tea or supper:
Green or Mixed Salad
Cheese Tomato Charlotte
Banana and Apple Jelly *page 72*
for lunch or dinner:
Orange and Grapefruit
Cocktail *page 13*
Cheese Tomato Charlotte
Salad or spinach
Potato Soufflé *page 60*
Banana and Apple Jelly *page 72*

4 large slices bread
2 oz. fat (margarine, or dripping)
10 oz. cheese (suitable for cooking, see page 58)
small can tomatoes
½–1 teaspoon made-mustard
seasoning
2 teaspoons chopped chives, or onion
1 teaspoon cornflour
5 tablespoons stock, or water and ½ teaspoon yeast extract
few drops Worcestershire sauce

Cut the bread into neat fingers, and fry in the hot fat until crisp on both sides. Grate or dice the cheese, put into a basin; add the very well-drained tomatoes, mustard, seasoning, chives or onion, blend well. Put the liquid from the can into a saucepan. Arrange half the bread in a shallow ovenproof dish. Top with the cheese mixture, and the remainder of the bread. Bake in the centre of a moderate to moderately hot oven, 375–400°F., Gas Mark 5–6, for 25–30 minutes. Meanwhile, blend the cornflour with the stock, or water and yeast extract. Add this and the Worcestershire sauce to the tomato liquid. Bring the sauce to the boil, stirring well, and cook until thickened slightly.

To make Pancakes

The batter given below is used for the Yorkshire pudding on page 37, and for pancakes. While plain flour is recommended, a satisfactory result will be obtained with self-raising flour. A lighter, but less nutritious mixture, is produced by using half milk and half water. You can make pancakes, but not a Yorkshire pudding, by omitting the egg.

To make the batter: sieve 4 oz. flour with a pinch salt, add 1 egg and beat well, then gradually beat in ½ pint milk, or milk and water. If allowed to stand, whisk sharply before using.

To make pancakes: heat about ½ oz. fat, or ½ tablespoon oil, in the frying pan; when hot, spoon in enough batter to give a paper-thin covering. Cook quickly until brown on the under-side; if the pancake moves easily in the pan it is ready to turn. Slip a broad-bladed knife or fish slice under the pancake, turn and cook on the second side for about 1 minute. Lift the pancake on to a plate, roll or fold. If filling, remove the pancake from the pan on to a plate, add the filling, roll or fold. As you cook the pancakes, keep them hot over a pan of boiling water, or in the oven — do not cover. Pancakes may be cooked ahead, separated with pieces of greaseproof paper, and wrapped in foil, then stored for several days in a refrigerator, or for some weeks in a home freezer. Reheat in the oven or pan.

Sweet pancakes: tip on to sugared paper, roll, and serve with lemon: fill with hot jam, or fruit purée, and roll.
Savoury pancakes: fill with cooked vegetables; a thick cheese sauce, see page 33; minced meat mixture, as page 43; or cooked chicken, or fish, in a white or cheese sauce, see page 33.
Pancakes au gratin: top filled pancakes with grated cheese and crumbs, or cheese sauce then cheese, etc. Brown in the oven.

Baked Omelette: melt 1 oz. margarine in an ovenproof dish; add 4 oz. cooked vegetables, heat for a few minutes. Beat 4 eggs with 2 tablespoons milk or water, and seasoning, pour over the vegetables and set for 15 minutes towards the top of a moderately hot oven. Serve with toast, or vegetables as a light main dish. Vary by adding cheese to the eggs. Serves 4.

Egg Fingers: beat and season 1 egg and 1 tablespoon milk, or water blended with ½ teaspoon Marmite. Soak 4 fingers of bread in this until all the egg is absorbed. Fry in hot bacon fat until golden. Serve with bacon. Makes 4 portions.

English Monkey: melt 1 oz. margarine in a pan, then add 2 tablespoons milk, 3 tablespoons soft crumbs, 2 beaten eggs, seasoning. Stir until the eggs begin to set, then add 1–2 oz. grated cheese, and continue cooking for about 2 minutes. Pile on hot buttered toast, and garnish with parsley. Serves 4.

Cauliflower Cheese Dip: ingredients as Curried dip below, but omit the curry powder and flavour with 1 teaspoon tomato ketchup, and 1 teaspoon Worcestershire sauce. Add about 3 tablespoons tiny raw cauliflower sprigs. Serves 4.

Cheese Eggs: coat 4–6 hard-boiled eggs with the cheese potato mixture below, fry until brown. Serves 4–6.

Cheese Potato Balls: blend 4 oz. finely grated Dutch Gouda cheese, seasoning, ½ oz. butter, and 1 egg yolk or small egg, into 1 lb. cooked mashed potatoes. Form into balls, roll in beaten egg or milk, then in crisp breadcrumbs, and fry until crisp and golden brown. Serves 4. See picture, page 19.

Cheese and Spinach Savoury: spread an ovenproof dish with 1 oz. butter, add 3 oz. thinly sliced Dutch Gouda cheese, and 4–6 oz. cooked and well-drained spinach. Break 4 eggs carefully over the spinach, season. Spoon 2 tablespoons thin cream or top of the milk over the eggs (add a little Worcestershire sauce to this, if wished), sprinkle 1 oz. grated Gouda cheese over the cream or milk. Bake above the centre of a hot oven for about 15 minutes. Serves 4.

Cheese Spread: blend 2 oz. margarine, 2 tablespoons top of the milk, squeeze lemon juice, seasoning, and 4 oz. grated Cheddar cheese. Add a grated carrot, or a little finely chopped celery, or watercress leaves. Use for topping biscuits or spreading on bread for sandwiches. The spreads and dips can 'use up' stale pieces of cheese.

Curd Cheese Spread: if milk becomes sour, strain through fine muslin or a sieve. Use the buttermilk for mixing scones, or even for pastry. Season the curds well. Add a small knob of margarine or butter, together with chopped chives, or any of the ingredients in the Cheese spread above.

Curried Dip: blend together 6 oz. grated cheese, 2 tablespoons salad dressing or mayonnaise, 1 teaspoon curry powder, 2 tablespoons sultanas, 2 tablespoons very finely chopped chives, or spring onions. Add just enough top of the milk to make a soft creamy consistency. Serve with raw carrots, pieces of celery, or potato crisps, as a 'dip'. Serves 4.

Penny-wise Ideas for Eggs and Cheese

VEGETABLE DISHES AND SALADS

preparation and cooking time

quick ☆☆☆

over ¾ hour but under 2 hours ☆☆

over 2 hours ☆

Make good use of the wonderful selection of vegetables and salad ingredients available. Root vegetables — swedes, parsnips and turnips (as well as potatoes) are excellent if parboiled, then roasted until brown. Peas, beans, lentils add protein to the diet. Cook potatoes in their jackets in a saucepan or steamer to avoid waste. Slice any left and fry as sauté potatoes, or use in salads.

Macédoine of Vegetables is made by dicing root vegetables, then cooking them in salted water in a tightly covered casserole in the oven, or a pan. Toss any left in mayonnaise; serve as Russian salad. Often frozen or canned vegetables are a wise economy, when fresh vegetables are scarce and expensive. Frozen, canned, as well as fresh peas, are given a new flavour if cooked the French way — put a layer of very damp outer lettuce leaves in a strong saucepan or casserole. Add peas, seasoning, a sliced onion, knob of margarine, and a covering of damp lettuce. Put the lid on the pan or casserole and cook slowly for 45 minutes to 1 hour. The lettuce may also be served as a vegetable. Shredded cabbage and sprouts can replace lettuce in salads; not only cheaper but very interesting, as page 67. Where a recipe mentions 'green salad' use just lettuce, watercress, cress and cucumber.

Sliced tomatoes can be served as a salad; add oil, vinegar, seasoning, pinch of sugar and chopped parsley.

Prepare sliced cucumber in the same way, adding chives as well as parsley. Store all vegetables in a cool place.

Creamed Spinach: freshly cooked, canned, or frozen spinach can be mixed with a little cream, or thick white sauce.

☆☆☆ Devilled Potato Salad

Preparation time: 15 minutes
Cooking time: 20–25 minutes
Serves 4–6

☆☆☆ **Suggested menu**
Lemon Soup *page 21*
Fish Caesar Salad *page 34*
Devilled Potato Salad
Gooseberry Creams *page 73*

1 lb. old or new potatoes
salt
3–4 tablespoons mayonnaise
½–1 teaspoon curry powder
shake cayenne pepper
shake black pepper
few drops Worcestershire sauce
parsley
few spring onions

Wash the potatoes well, but do not peel or skin. Either boil in salted water, or lightly sprinkle with salt and steam over boiling water until just soft. Remove peel or skins while warm, and dice or slice the potatoes. Blend the mayonnaise with the curry powder, peppers, and sauce, then mix with the warm potatoes, a little chopped parsley and chopped onions. Put into a bowl, and top with more parsley and the chopped green stalks of the onions. Serve warm or cold.

To vary
a) Omit the curry powder.
b) Use oil and vinegar as a dressing instead of mayonnaise.
c) Add diced celery, and/or a few capers, and/or sliced gherkins or cucumber to the potatoes.
d) To serve as a hot salad, peel or skin the potatoes *before* cooking. Make the salad as above, and top with 'snippets' of fried or grilled bacon, or sliced hot Frankfurter sausages.

1½ lb. old potatoes
seasoning
1 oz. margarine
2 tablespoons milk

2 teaspoons chopped parsley, or
  ½ teaspoon dried parsley
1 teaspoon chopped mint, or
  pinch dried mint

Savoury Potatoes ☆☆☆

Preparation time: 10 minutes
Cooking time: 25 minutes
Serves 4

Suggested menu ☆☆
Herbed Lamb and
Tomato Stew *page 42*
Macédoine of Vegetables
page 66
Savoury Potatoes
Mocha Pudding *page 76*

Peel the potatoes and put into boiling salted water. Cook steadily until soft. Do not boil potatoes too rapidly, otherwise they break on the outside before they are cooked in the middle. Strain the potatoes, return to the pan, mash with a fork, then beat in the margarine, milk, herbs and extra seasoning. Continue beating until light and fluffy.

To vary

a) *Cheese Potatoes:* as savoury potatoes, but omit the herbs. Add 2 or 3 oz. grated, or diced, cheese to the mashed potatoes. Children generally love this.

b) *Duchesse Potatoes:* cook the potatoes, mash, then add 1–2 oz. margarine or butter. Add 1–2 egg yolks, seasoning, and beat well. Duchesse potatoes are generally piped into shapes, or made into an 'edging'; and milk causes the mixture to 'flop'. Pipe into 'rosettes' on a greased baking tin and brown in the oven, or pipe, or spread as a border round a dish, then brown under the grill or in the oven. Although not essential to use egg white, the potatoes will have an attractive shine if brushed with this before browning.

c) *Creamed Potatoes:* as savoury potatoes, but omit the herbs and add a little top of the milk or cream.

d) *Mashed Potatoes:* as savoury potatoes, but omit herbs.

e) *Potato Nests:* as savoury potatoes, but omit milk and herbs. Form the potato mixture into nest shapes on a well-greased oven-proof dish. Brush with a little milk, or beaten egg, or melted margarine, to encourage browning. Brown in the oven and fill with cooked vegetable, or a cheese sauce, see page 33.

f) Use instant dehydrated potatoes instead of fresh.

¼–½ small white cabbage, or
  cabbage heart
2–3 large carrots
1 dessert apple (optional)

1–2 sticks celery
2–3 tablespoons mayonnaise
1–2 teaspoons vinegar
little chopped parsley

Carrot Coleslaw ☆☆☆

Preparation time: 10 minutes
Cooking time: none
Serves 4–6

Suggested menu ☆
Beef Indienne *page 46*
Savoury Rice *page 56*
Carrot Coleslaw
Orange Sponge Pudding
page 75

Shred cabbage finely, then coarsely grate the peeled carrots and apple (do not prepare apple until ready to mix with the mayonnaise). Chop the celery finely. Blend the mayonnaise, vinegar and parsley in a bowl. Add the rest of the ingredients, and stir thoroughly. Allow to stand a short time before the meal, if possible.

To vary

a) Omit carrots, add a little chopped onion if desired.

b) Add pinch cinnamon and a little mustard to the mayonnaise.

DESSERTS AND PUDDINGS

preparation and cooking time

quick ☆☆☆

over ¾ hour but ☆☆
under 2 hours

over 2 hours ☆

Many puddings can be quite inexpensive as well as interesting, and a selection are given in this chapter. Some of these are 'basic' recipes that you can vary, using different kinds of fruit throughout the year.

Try to choose your pudding to 'fit in' with the main dish, i.e. if most of the meal is cooked in the oven you will save money on fuel if you select a pudding that is baked; if the main course, etc., is cooked on top of the cooker then try to avoid heating the oven merely to cook the pudding.

Choose a pudding or dessert that supplements the food values of the rest of the meal, as follows:

If your meal does not include fresh green vegetables, then it is wise to have a pudding or dessert that includes citrus fruits, or those fruits rich in Vitamin C, i.e. blackcurrants and strawberries. Remember this vitamin is destroyed by cooking, so try to have raw fruit, or flavour a fruit salad with orange juice, or make a fruit sauce, see page 74.

'Milky' puddings are an excellent way to make sure that children, who perhaps do not drink sufficient milk, have this important food in an appetising manner. Eggs, when used in a pudding or dessert, add extra protein to the meal.

The pudding or dessert should be chosen carefully to give a well-balanced meal. If the meal starter and main courses are substantial, then the dessert should be light and refreshing. On the other hand, if you have a light salad as a main course, you produce a more satisfying meal if this is followed by a fairly substantial hot pudding. Do not repeat flavours, that is, if serving pork and apple sauce avoid an apple dessert or pudding.

Choosing wisely

Milk is economical and nourishing, so use it to make jellies, blanc-mange, etc. Instructions are on the packet for most puddings, but when making a *Milk jelly* dissolve a fruit-flavoured tablet in ¼ pint very hot water; cool, then add ¾ pint cold milk. This prevents the jelly curdling. Another 'old fashioned' dessert with milk is a *Junket*. Warm 1 pint pasteurised milk to blood heat, add sugar to taste then 2 teaspoons rennet, and allow to clot.

Cream is not very cheap for desserts, so use evaporated milk or Dream Topping. To *whip evaporated milk* – boil the can in a pan of water for 15 minutes, cool, open and whip.

If you use half thick and half thin cream you produce a light consistency. Whip the thick cream until it begins to hold its shape, then gradually whisk in the thin cream. Another way to make thick cream 'go further' is to add 1 stiffly beaten egg white to each ¼ pint whipped cream.

Apples are an economical fruit, and several desserts using these are in this section. Buy 'loose' good quality *bananas*, rather than those on a bunch, to save a little money.

4 oz. flour, preferably plain
pinch salt
1 egg
¼ pint milk
3 tablespoons water

1 large cooking apple
1 oz. fat
2 tablespoons golden syrup,
   honey, or brown sugar

Apple Puffs ☆☆☆

Preparation time: 10–15 minutes
Cooking time: 18 minutes
Makes 12

Suggested menu ☆☆
Curried Vegetable Soup *page 17*
Polish Chicken Salad *page 49*
Speedy Rolls *page 16*
Apple Puffs

Sieve the flour and salt. Add the egg, and some of the milk, and beat well until smooth. Whisk in the remainder of the milk and water. Peel and core the apple; cut into tiny pieces, add to the batter. Divide the fat between 12 patty tins. Heat for a few minutes in a hot oven. Spoon mixture into tins and bake for about 15 minutes towards the top of a hot oven, 425°F., Gas Mark 6–7. Turn out, top with warmed syrup, or honey, or sprinkle with sugar. Serve hot.

To vary
a) Omit the apple; add the grated rind of 1–2 oranges and blend the batter with the milk and 4 tablespoons orange juice, or use diluted orange squash and omit the grated rind.
b) Omit the apple; use 4 tablespoons water and add 2 oz. sultanas to the batter.
c) Make savoury puffs; season the batter well, add (1) 2 oz. finely grated cheese, or (2) 2 oz. diced cooked meat.
Bake as above, and top with heated baked beans or cooked vegetables.

¼ pint water
2–3 oz. sugar
1 lb. cooking apples*
8 oz. raspberries

for the cobbler
4 oz. flour (with plain flour use
   1 teaspoon baking powder)
1 oz. margarine
1 oz. sugar
milk to mix

Apple and Raspberry Cobbler ☆☆

Preparation time: 20 minutes
Cooking time: 30 minutes
Serves 4–6

Suggested menu ☆☆
Spinach Soup *page 22*
Viennese Steaks with fried onions *page 53*
Green Salad *page 66*
Creamed Potatoes (optional)
Apple and Raspberry Cobbler

See picture, *page 59*

* apples are a very pleasant fruit, and they also 'bring out' the flavour of other fruit. A cobbler is an economical topping.

Put the water and sugar into a saucepan. Stir until the sugar has dissolved, bring to the boil. Add the sliced peeled apples, and allow to simmer for about 10 minutes. Add the raspberries and transfer to a pie dish. Prepare the cobbler mixture while the fruit cooks, and make sure the oven is becoming hot. Sieve the flour, or flour and baking powder. Rub in the margarine, add the sugar, and mix to a soft rolling consistency with the milk. Roll out to ½ inch in thickness, cut into triangles or rounds. Put on top of the *hot* fruit, and bake above the centre of a hot to very hot oven, 450–475°F., Gas Mark 7–8, for about 12–15 minutes. Serve hot or cold, but eat when fresh.
Note. All fruit can be served this way.

Banana Fritters

☆☆☆

Preparation time: 10 minutes
Cooking time: 8 or 5 minutes
Serves 4–6

☆☆☆ **Suggested menu**
Ham and Green Pea Chowder
page 14
Cold Meat and Mixed Salad
Banana Fritters

4 oz. flour (with plain flour use
 1 teaspoon baking powder)
pinch salt
1 egg
¼ pint milk, or milk and water
4–6 bananas
1 level tablespoon flour

for frying
fat or oil

to coat
1–2 oz. sugar

Make a thick batter of 4 oz. flour, salt, egg and milk, or milk and water. Roll the peeled, halved, bananas in the extra flour, coat with batter. Fry in shallow fat for about 8 minutes, turning, until golden brown, or for 4–5 minutes in deep fat. Drain on absorbent paper and roll in sugar.

Orange Fritters

☆☆☆

Preparation time: 10 minutes
Cooking time: 5 minutes
Serves 4

☆☆☆ **Suggested menu**
Haddock Belle Bretonne
page 29
Fresh, frozen, or canned peas,
or green vegetable
Creamed Potatoes, use fresh or
instant potatoes
Orange Fritters

1–2 oranges
1 egg yolk
4 tablespoons milk
8 slices bread

3 oz. margarine
2–3 tablespoons orange
 marmalade
little sugar

Grate the rind from the oranges, blend with the egg yolk and milk, and pour on to a large flat dish. Make sandwiches with the bread, 1 oz. of the margarine, and the marmalade. Cut into neat fingers (remove crusts if wished). Heat the remaining margarine in a large frying pan. Soak the sandwich fingers in the egg yolk mixture for ½–1 minute only, turn and soak on the second side for the same time, then fry until crisp and brown on one side. Turn and fry on the other side. Lift on to a hot dish, top with the sugar and keep hot until ready to serve. Either cut away the orange peel, divide the oranges into segments, and pile on the fritters, or, squeeze the juice from the oranges and pour this on the fritters, just before serving.

To vary
a) Use jam in place of marmalade, and flavour the egg and milk with a pinch of mixed spice, or a few drops vanilla essence.
b) Substitute orange juice or squash for the milk.

Oranged bananas

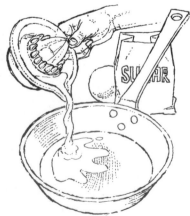

Put the juice of 2 large oranges and 2 oz. sugar into a large frying pan.

Stir over a low heat until the sugar has melted.

Add 4–6 peeled small bananas and turn in the orange syrup until coated.

3 oz. sugar
½ pint water

1 lb. *prepared* fruit
    (apples, plums, etc.)
flavourings, see method

Heat the sugar and water in a saucepan, or in a casserole. If you heat the sugar and water syrup first, the fruit keeps a better shape. Put in the fruit and simmer gently until tender: or, if using a casserole, cover with foil, or a lid, and cook in the coolest part of a very moderate or moderate oven, 325° or 350–375°F., Gas Mark 3 or 4–5, until tender. Naturally fruit varies considerably in the time it takes to cook, but sliced apples take from 10 minutes simmering in a saucepan, or about 30 minutes in a casserole in a very moderate oven. If you choose economical fruit in season you can vary this with different flavourings: *apples* can be flavoured with grated lemon rind and juice, or chopped dates, or sultanas, or ginger.
plums are good with cinnamon, or pieces orange rind.

Preparation time:
10–20 minutes
Cooking time: see method
Serves 4

Suggested menu ☆☆
Baked Sausages in Cider
page 39
Bacon Jacket Potatoes *page 41*
Tomato Salad *page 66*
Compôte of Fruit

These can be made in so many different ways:
a) Open a can of fruit, add as much diced, or sliced, fresh fruit as you require.
b) Make a flavoured syrup by simmering the thinly pared rind from 1–2 oranges in ½ pint water for about 10 minutes. Add 2–3 oz. sugar to the liquid, which will become just over ¼ pint. Strain, and pour over the mixed fresh fruit.
c) Mix fresh fruit with compôte of fruit.

Do not imagine one has to have a very wide range of fruits — some delicious salads are (1) melon and orange; (2) apple and banana; (3) orange and peeled fresh chestnuts (simmered in syrup until tender); (4) cooked prunes and fresh apples; (5) grapefruit, orange, or tangerine, and chopped nuts.

Fruit Salads

---

3 oz. round (short grain) rice
1 pint milk
2 oz. sugar
¼ pint thick cream

small can pineapple rings
1 teaspoon arrowroot, or
    cornflour
2 tablespoons apricot jam

Pineapple ☆☆☆
Condé

Cook the rice in the milk with the sugar in a strong pan, until it is tender and the mixture is the consistency of thick cream. It takes longer to cook the rice in the top of a double saucepan but this prevents any possibility of it burning. Allow to cool, then fold in the whipped cream. Put into a dish. Top with the well-drained rings of pineapple. Blend ¼ pint syrup from the can with the arrowroot or cornflour. Put into a saucepan with the jam, and stir over a gentle heat until thickened and clear. Cool slightly, then spoon over the pineapple.

Preparation time: 15 minutes
Cooking time: 30 minutes
Serves 4–5

Suggested menu ☆☆
Fish Cakes *page 35*
with Tartare Sauce *page 52*
Macédoine of Vegetables
page 66
Pineapple Condé

Banana and Apple Jelly

Preparation time: 10 minutes
Cooking time: few minutes
Serves 4

 Suggested menus
for high tea or supper:
Cheese Tomato Charlotte
page 64
Green or Mixed Salad
Banana and Apple Jelly
for lunch or dinner:
Orange and Grapefruit Cocktail
page 13
Salad or spinach
Potato Soufflé *page 60*
Banana and Apple Jelly

1 lemon-flavoured jelly	2 medium dessert apples
¾ pint water less 2 tablespoons	2 medium bananas

Dissolve the jelly in the very hot water. Allow to cool. Peel, and grate the apples into the jelly, then add the sliced bananas. Pour into a mould or basin rinsed in cold water, and allow to set. Turn out: the apples and bananas will then be at the top of the jelly when serving. If you wish the fruit mixed evenly throughout the jelly, stir once or twice as the jelly sets.

To vary

a) *Raisin and Apple Jelly:* omit the bananas. Add 2–3 oz. seedless raisins to the hot liquid jelly, allow to cool then add the grated apple.
b) *Banana Cream Jelly:* dissolve the jelly in just ¾ pint hot water. Cool, then pour gradually on to 2 mashed bananas. Allow to set lightly, then fold in ¼ pint whipped thick cream.

 # Rhubarb Whip

Preparation time: 15 minutes
Cooking time: 15 minutes
Serves 4–5

 Suggested menu
Viennese Boat *page 41*
Mixed Salad, or Coleslaw
page 67
Rhubarb Whip

1 lb. rhubarb	½ oz. powdered gelatine
¼ pint water	3 tablespoons thin cream
2–3 oz. sugar	2 egg whites

Cut the rhubarb into neat pieces and cook with the water (except 2 tablespoons) and sugar, until very soft. Sieve or beat to make a smooth purée. Check to see you have just ¾ pint purée; if too little, add enough water to make this amount; if too much, then use any surplus as a sauce with the dessert. Soften the gelatine in the remaining water, stir into the hot fruit purée, and continue stirring until dissolved. Cool slightly and add the cream; then allow the mixture to become quite cold and nearly stiff. Tip into a basin and whisk hard; then fold in the firmly beaten egg whites. Spoon into a dish or glasses.

To vary

a) *Apple and Orange Whip:* use cooking apples in place of rhubarb, and flavour with the finely grated rind of 1–2 oranges. Use the orange juice in place of some of the water.
b) *Berry Whip:* use gooseberries, blackberries, etc., in place of rhubarb.

To whisk an egg white

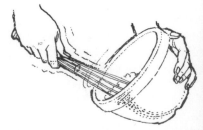

Make sure the basin is free from grease. Separate the egg yolk and white.

Whisk sharply until the white is very stiff.

1 lb. ripe gooseberries
¼ pint water
3 oz. sugar
2 teaspoons powdered gelatine

1 level tablespoon custard powder
½ pint milk
¼ pint thick cream

Gooseberry Creams ☆☆☆

Preparation time: 20 minutes
Cooking time: 15–20 minutes
Serves 4–6

Suggested menu ☆☆☆
Lemon Soup *page 21*
Fish Caesar Salad *page 34*
Devilled Potato Salad *page 66*
Gooseberry Creams

If you intend sieving the gooseberries there is no need to 'top and tail' them. If you are using an electric liquidiser, or are just beating the fruit, then remove the stalk and flower ends with scissors. Put the washed fruit, nearly all the water, and 2 oz. sugar, into a saucepan. Cover the pan and cook until the fruit is very soft. Sieve the purée, if wished, and return to the pan or beat hard with a wooden spoon. Soften the gelatine in the remaining cold water, stir into the warm fruit purée, and continue stirring over a gentle heat until the gelatine is thoroughly dissolved. Make a smooth thick custard with the powder, milk and remaining sugar. If you have a liquidiser, put the fruit purée and the custard into the warmed goblet and emulsify together. If you have beaten or sieved the fruit, then whisk the custard in until well blended. Whip the cream until it stands up in peaks. Allow the fruit mixture to cool, then fold in half the whipped cream. Spoon into dishes and decorate with the rest of the whipped cream.

To vary
a) Use any other fruit required. With very firm fruit use an extra 5–6 tablespoons water.
b) Top with chopped nuts and/or glacé cherries.
c) Turn into a fruit trifle: put 3–4 sponge cakes into a dish; add the jellied fruit, allow to cool, then top with the cool custard. (You may like to use a double quantity of custard.) Decorate with the whipped cream. Serves 6–8.

1 lemon
1 lemon-flavoured jelly
2 eggs

1 oz. sugar
¼ pint thick cream, or whipped evaporated milk, see page 68

Lemon Soufflé ☆☆☆

Preparation time: 10 minutes
Cooking time: 10 minutes
Serves 4–6

Suggested menu ☆☆
Rillette of Chicken *page 10*
French Peas *page 66*
Duchesse Potatoes *page 67*
Lemon Soufflé

See picture, *page 63*

Cut away the top lemon rind, simmer with ½ pint water for 10 minutes, strain and dissolve the lemon jelly in this. Add the lemon juice and enough cold water to make up to ¾ pint. Separate the eggs, beat the yolks and sugar, add the lemon liquid, allow to stiffen slightly, then add half the whipped cream, or evaporated milk, and stiffly beaten egg whites. Put into a suitable dish, and when set, top with the remainder of the whipped cream, or evaporated milk.

To vary
a) *Orange Soufflé:* use an orange and orange-flavoured jelly.
b) *Chocolate Soufflé:* dissolve ½ oz. powder gelatine and 2 oz. sweetened chocolate powder in ¼ pint water, then make as above.

Coconut Plum Dumplings

Preparation time: 10 minutes
Cooking time: 35 minutes
Serves 4

☆☆☆ **Suggested menu**
Melon Cocktail *page 9*
Chicken and Ham Supreme
page 47
Herbed Rice *page 56*
Green Vegetable
Coconut Plum Dumplings

8 ripe but firm plums
3 oz. sugar
8 oz. flour (with plain flour use
2 level teaspoons baking
powder)
pinch salt
2 oz. shredded suet
2 oz. desiccated coconut
water to mix

Stone the plums if it is possible to do this without spoiling the fruit. If you have removed the stone, fill the cavity with a little sugar and press the two halves together. Sieve the flour, or flour and baking powder, with the salt. Add the suet, 1½ oz. sugar and half the coconut. Mix to a pliable dough with water; roll out to about ¼ inch thick, and cut into squares. Bring approximately 2 pints of water to the boil in a large saucepan before completing the dumplings. Wrap each plum in a square of pastry, and press this round the fruit. Put the dumplings into the boiling water and cook for about 25 minutes. Lift out with a perforated spoon, put on to a serving dish, and top with sugar and coconut.

To vary

a) *Czech Dumplings:* stone the plums and fill with cream cheese; press the two halves together.
b) Omit the coconut in the dumplings, and dust with sugar and grated nutmeg.
c) Use a little fruit juice, or fruit syrup (from a can or from cooking fruit), to flavour the water in which the dumplings are cooked.

Halfpay Pudding

Preparation time:
10–15 minutes
Cooking time: 1½–2 hours
Serves 4–6

☆ **Suggested menu**
Stuffed Herrings *page 28*
Potato Salad *page 66*
Tomato Salad *page 66*
Halfpay Pudding

3 oz. shredded suet, or
margarine
4 oz. breadcrumbs
2 oz. flour (with plain flour use
1 level teaspoon baking
powder)
5 tablespoons golden syrup
3 oz. sultanas
3 oz. currants
milk to mix

Mix together the suet, crumbs and sieved flour, or flour and baking powder. If using margarine, melt this and add in place of the suet. Add 2 tablespoons of the golden syrup, then the dried fruit, and mix thoroughly. Stir in enough milk to give a sticky consistency. Put the rest of the syrup into a greased basin, add the mixture, cover with greased paper or foil, and steam for 1½–2 hours.

To vary

a) Omit syrup in the basin, and serve with *Fresh Fruit Sauce:* blend ½ tablespoon cornflour, grated rind 2 oranges or lemons, ½ pint water and 2–3 oz. sugar. Cook until thickened, then add the fruit juice – do not reheat.
b) *Jam Cap Pudding:* omit fruit and syrup from the recipe above, add 2–3 oz. sugar in the pudding, and put jam in the basin.

2 oranges
3 oz. margarine
2 oz. sugar
5 tablespoons orange marmalade
1 egg

6 oz. self-raising flour (or plain flour and 1½ level teaspoons baking powder)
3 tablespoons milk

Orange Sponge Pudding

Preparation time: 20 minutes
Cooking time: 1½ hours
Serves 4—6

Suggested menu ☆

Beef Indienne *page 46*
Savoury Rice *page 56*
Carrot Coleslaw *page 67*
Orange Sponge Pudding

Grate the rind from the oranges and put into a mixing bowl with the margarine, sugar, and 2 tablespoons marmalade. Cream until soft and light. Add the egg, and beat well, then fold in the sieved flour, or flour and baking powder, and milk. Cut away the peel from the oranges, then slice the fruit. Remove any pips. Put the rest of the marmalade into the bottom of a greased 2-pint basin, then arrange the orange slices round the sides of the basin. Put in the sponge mixture. Cover with greased greaseproof paper and foil. Steam over boiling water for 1½ hours. Turn out carefully.

To vary

a) *Pineapple Sponge:* use well-drained pineapple rings instead of oranges.
b) *Jam Sponge:* use jam, or golden syrup, in the basin and to mix the pudding — omit sliced oranges and marmalade.
c) *Lemon Sponge:* use lemon marmalade in the pudding and basin— omit sliced oranges.

---

for the caramel
4 oz. sugar
3 tablespoons water
1 pint milk

2 large slices bread
2 eggs or 2 egg yolks
1 oz. glacé cherries
1 oz. walnuts (optional)

Caramel Pudding

Preparation time: 15 minutes
Cooking time: 1¼ hours
Serves 5—6

Suggested menu ☆

Spanish Beef Casserole
page 42
Jacket Potatoes *page 41*
Green Vegetable
Caramel Pudding

Put 3 oz. sugar and the water into a strong saucepan. Stir until the sugar has dissolved, then boil steadily until a golden brown caramel. Remove the pan from the heat and allow the caramel to cool slightly. Add the milk and heat *gently*, stirring from time to time until the milk absorbs the caramel. Cut the bread into small cubes, put into a basin. Beat the eggs, or egg yolks, with the remaining sugar, and add to the caramel liquid. Whisk together, then pour over the bread and leave to soak for about 15 minutes. Add the chopped cherries and chopped nuts, then spoon into a 2—3-pint pie dish or ovenproof dish. Stand in a tin of cold water (to prevent the pudding curdling) and bake for 1 hour in the centre of a very moderate oven, 325°F., Gas Mark 3. Serve hot.

To vary

a) Add 2 oz. sultanas to the bread, etc.
b) Make the bread into crumbs, instead of cutting it into cubes.
c) If more convenient, bake the pudding for 1¼—1½ hours in a slow oven.

Mocha Pudding

Preparation time: 10 minutes
Cooking time: 10 minutes
Serves 4

 Suggested menu
Herbed Lamb and Tomato Stew
page 42
Savoury Potatoes *page 67*
Macédoine of Vegetables
page 66
Mocha Pudding

2 oz. sultanas
½ pint moderately strong coffee
1 chocolate blancmange
　powder
½ pint milk
2 oz. sugar
1 oz. chopped walnuts

Put the sultanas into a basin; heat some of the coffee, pour over the fruit and leave for a few minutes. Blend the blancmange powder with the cold coffee. Heat the milk, pour over the blancmange powder, and blend very carefully. Return to the pan, with the sultanas and coffee from the basin, and the sugar. Bring slowly to the boil, stirring well until mixture thickens. Continue to cook for 2 or 3 minutes. Rinse out a mould, or basin, with cold water. Pour in chocolate and coffee mixture, and leave to set. Turn out, top with chopped walnuts.

To vary
a) Use 1 oz. plain cornflour and ½ oz. cocoa instead of a chocolate blancmange.
b) Add a few drops of rum essence, or a good tablespoon rum, to the sultanas and coffee. If using rum use ½ pint *less* 1 tablespoon coffee or milk.
c) For special occasions: use rum as b), and ¼ pint very strong coffee, ½ pint milk *less* 1 tablespoon, ¼ pint thin cream.

Date and Apple Crisp

Preparation time: 15 minutes
Cooking time: 40 minutes
Serves 4

 **Suggested menu**
Sardine Salad *page 11*
Farmhouse Pie *page 61*
Brussels sprouts, or other green
vegetable
Date and Apple Crisp

1 lb. cooking apples* (weight
　when peeled)
3 tablespoons water
1–2 oz. sugar
2–4 oz. cooking dates

for the topping
2 oz. margarine
1 tablespoon golden syrup
1 oz. sugar
4 oz. quick-cooking rolled oats

* or use canned apple pie filling, and omit water and sugar.

Core, and slice or chop the apples neatly. Simmer for about 10 minutes with the water and sugar, then add the chopped dates and put into a 1½–2-pint pie dish. Melt the margarine with the golden syrup and sugar; add the rolled oats. Spread this mixture on top of the apples. Smooth flat with a damp palette knife. Bake for approximately 30 minutes in the centre of a moderate oven, 350–375°F., Gas Mark 4–5.
Note. The topping is as a flapjack biscuit; so you can make a double quantity, use half for a pudding and bake the rest separately, see Apple Flapjack, page 78.

To vary
Any fruit can be used instead of apples and dates, but make certain it is not too soft, otherwise the topping will not become crisp; and could 'fall' into the fruit.
Syrup Crumble Mixture: cream margarine, syrup and sugar, as recipe, add 4 oz. flour instead of oats. Continue as above.

short crust pastry

6 oz. flour, preferably plain
pinch salt
3 oz. margarine, or 1½ oz.
    margarine and 1½ oz. cooking
    fat
cold water to mix

for the filling

1 oz. butter, or margarine
2 oz. Demerara sugar
1 level tablespoon golden syrup
1 egg
¼ pint evaporated milk

Gypsy Tart ☆☆

Preparation time: 25 minutes
Cooking time: 35—40 minutes
Serves 4—6

Suggested menu ☆☆

Herring Bake *page 29*
Jacket Potatoes *page 41*
Spinach
Gypsy Tart

See picture, *page 63*

Sieve the flour and salt, rub in the margarine, or mixture of fats, until like fine breadcrumbs, see sketch below. Add sufficient cold water (approximately 1½ tablespoons) to bind. Gather the pastry into a 'ball' and roll out until about ¼ inch in thickness. Line either an 8-inch flan ring (on an upturned baking tray) or a sandwich tin, with pastry, see below. Put greased greaseproof paper, and crusts of bread or haricot beans, into the pastry case; bake 'blind' for approximately 15 minutes in the centre of a hot oven, 425—450°F., Gas Mark 6—7, until set and pale golden. Lift the flan out of the oven, remove the paper, etc., and the flan ring, but do not try and turn out of a sandwich tin. Lower the heat to very moderate, 325—350°F., Gas Mark 3—4. Put in the filling. To make this, cream the butter, sugar and golden syrup, add the egg, beat well, then gradually blend in the evaporated milk. Pour into the pastry case and continue cooking until firm. Allow to cool.

To vary Pastry

Sweet Short Crust: ingredients as short crust pastry above, but add 1 tablespoon sugar to the flour. Bake at a slightly lower temperature, i.e. 25°F. or 1 Gas Mark, than short crust.
Cheese Pastry: omit 1 oz. fat from short crust pastry above, season the flour well. Add 2 oz. finely grated Cheddar cheese. Bind with egg yolk and water, or water. Bake as sweet short crust. This is an ideal cheese pastry for pies etc., see page 61.
Economical Pastry: use only 2—3 oz. fat to 8 oz. *self-raising* flour, or use 4 oz. self-raising flour and 4 oz. mashed potato. Eat when fresh.

Note. When a recipe says 4 oz. short crust pastry it means pastry made with 4 oz. flour etc.

Tips when making pastry

Rub the fat into the flour with the tips of your fingers.

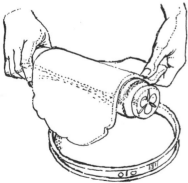

Support the pastry over the rolling pin when putting into the flan case etc.

Roll or cut the edges — rolling is quicker.

When baking 'blind', fill with paper etc., see above, to prevent pastry rising.

Penny-wise Ideas for Desserts and Puddings

Use canned fruit pie fillings when fresh fruit is expensive. This is excellent in pies, tarts, and as a sauce for puddings.

Apple Flapjack: prepare the topping mixture as the Date and Apple Crisp, page 76. Spread into a well-greased 7-inch sandwich tin, and bake for 25 minutes in the centre of a moderate oven. When cooked, mark in sections, allow to cool and top each one with thick apple purée *just before serving*. Serves 4.

Baked Custard: beat 2 eggs (or use egg yolks only and save the whites for the Rhubarb Whip, page 72) with 1 oz. sugar. Add 1 pint warm milk. Strain into a pie dish, top with grated nutmeg and stand in a tin of cold water. Bake for $1-1\frac{1}{4}$ hours in the centre of a slow oven until firm. Vary by adding a little chocolate powder, or coffee essence, to the eggs. Serves 4.

Crumb Trifle: make 1 pint sweetened custard as instructed on packet. Blend in 3 oz. fine sweet biscuit, or sponge crumbs. Spoon into dish; cool. Spread with jam and lightly whipped cream, or Dream Topping; decorate with glacé cherries. Serves 4–5.

Fruit Charlotte: cook 1 lb. apples, rhubarb, or other fruit, with the minimum of water and sugar to taste. Toss 6 oz. coarse breadcrumbs in 2 oz. margarine until coated, or mix with 2 oz. shredded suet. Add 2 oz. brown sugar. Put one-third of the crumb mixture into an oven-proof dish, add half the fruit, a third of the crumbs, then the fruit, top with crumbs. Bake in the centre of a very moderate oven for 35–40 minutes. Serves 4–5.

Glazed Fruit Fool: cook 1 lb. prepared gooseberries, or other fruit, with just *over* $\frac{1}{2}$ pint water and 2–3 oz. sugar, until soft. Strain off juice; sieve or beat the fruit until smooth, blend with $\frac{1}{2}$ pint thick custard. Spoon into a dish and cool. Meanwhile dissolve half a fruit-flavoured jelly in the fruit syrup, cool, and wait until this just begins to stiffen, then spoon over the Fruit Fool, and leave until set. Serves 4–5.

Pain Perdu: cut 8 fingers of white bread about $\frac{3}{4}$ inch thick and 2 inches wide. Beat 1 egg with 1 oz. sugar and 2 tablespoons thin cream, or inexpensive white wine. Soak the fingers in this mixture, fry until golden. Mix 2 oz. sugar with $\frac{1}{2}$ teaspoon powdered cinnamon, sprinkle over the fingers. Serves 4.

Stuffed Baked Apples: core 4 medium cooking apples, slit the skins round the middle. Put into baking dish. Fill centres with a) brown sugar and sultanas, b) bramble jelly, c) golden syrup. Bake for about 1 hour in a moderate oven. Serves 4.

Ice Cream Sundaes: top ice cream with a) fruit or fruit purée and cream, b) chocolate sauce (melt plain chocolate with a few drops of water in a basin over boiling water), and chopped nuts or pears, c) hot fudge sauce made by melting fudge as the chocolate sauce above, add chopped walnuts or d) add evaporated milk to cool lime jelly; crumble chocolate biscuits, see picture, page 63.

Custard Cream: make 1 pint thick sweetened custard sauce as directions on packet. Dissolve 2 level teaspoons powdered gelatine in the hot custard. Cool, stirring from time to time to prevent skin forming. Fold in $\frac{1}{4}$ pint whipped cream. Serves 4.

Fruit Cups: as Custard Cream plus $\frac{1}{2}-\frac{3}{4}$ pint fruit purée. Put a layer of purée into dishes. Spoon Custard Cream mixture over the fruit. When cool top with fruit purée. Serves 5–6.

INDEX